Language Connections

Language Connections

Writing and Reading across the Curriculum

Edited by

Toby Fulwiler
Michigan Technological University

Art Young
Michigan Technological University

National Council of Teachers of English
1111 Kenyon Road, Urbana, Illinois 61801

Portions of "Cross-Disciplinary Writing Programs: Beginnings" by Randall Freisinger first appeared in "Cross-Disciplinary Writing Workshops: Theory and Practice," *College English* 42 (October 1980). Portions of "The Personal Connection: Journal Writing across the Curriculum" by Toby Fulwiler first appeared in Gene Stanford, chair, and the NCTE Committee on Classroom Practices, "Journal Writing across the Curriculum," *Classroom Practices in Teaching English, 1979–1980: How to Handle the Paper Load* (NCTE, 1979) and in "Journals across the Disciplines," *English Journal* 69 (December 1980). Portions of "Assigning and Evaluating Transactional Writing," by Toby Fulwiler and Robert Jones and portions of "Talking about Writing: The Role of the Language Lab" by Diana Freisinger and Jill Burkland first appeared in *Evaluating a Theme,* edited by Rhoda Maxwell and Stephen Judy (MCTE Annual Yearbook, 1981).

Book Design: Tom Kovacs

NCTE Stock Number 26537

Library of Congress Cataloging in Publication Data
Main entry under title:

Language connections.

  Bibliography: p.
  1. English language—Rhetoric—Addresses,
essays, lectures. 2. Universities and colleges—
United States—Curricula—Addresses, essays,
lectures. I. Fulwiler, Toby, 1942–   .
II. Young, Art, 1943–   . II. National Council
of Teachers of English.
LB2365.E5L3   378'.199   82-3468
ISBN 0-8141-2653-7   AACR2

Contents

Foreword

I was intrigued to receive from an American publisher the other day instructions to authors which included the information that I might quote, free of charge, a passage of 150 words from a text in the humanities, but only 50 words from a scientific text. So there *are* modes of writing appropriate to different disciplines and they even have a commercial rating in the eyes of the law! When university subject specialists and language specialists get together to consider these modes of writing appropriate to the various disciplines, we may hope to learn a great deal we don't know today, not in crude terms of commercial value, but in terms of the learning strategies by which specialist knowledge is generated and the strategies by which it is communicated. As I read the chapters of this book, it seemed to me that the off-campus writing workshops (a feature of the cross-disciplinary program from which the book was written) promised real progress in this direction.

As I see it, the message of this book lies above all in what it implies about *learning*. No one who reads it with understanding can continue to confuse rote learning with real learning—however deeply engrained that confusion is in our current modes of teaching and assessment.

This is a pioneer effort: the work of my colleagues and myself in London University has been widely taken up and applied in elementary and secondary schools, but there has hitherto been very little evidence of impact upon universities. Because this book both pursues theoretical issues and speaks from first-hand experience of their applications to practice, I believe it will be influential both in universities and in schools. I have read it with a growing respect for the enterprise that lies behind it, and the invitation to write this brief foreword is therefore a source of pride and pleasure to me.

James Britton

Introduction

Many schools lack a comprehensive literate environment which encourages good writing and reading habits. Without such an environment, students are not compelled to take writing and reading seriously. In schools where the lessons taught in English classes are not repeated and emphasized in the student's other classes, the knowledge and skills learned in those lessons tends to atrophy. We believe language skills deserve more conscious attention from teachers in all academic disciplines, and that teachers who recognize the role played by these "elementary" skills can help students increase their learning ability, improve their communication skills, and enhance their cognitive and emotional growth.

Our aim in this book is not to make every teacher an expert in writing and reading. We believe English teachers have unique and specialized contributions to make in the education of students; the complex and difficult techniques for teaching traditional and transformational grammar, rhetorical conventions, and discourse theory remain in their domain. However, teachers in disciplines other than English can draw on general language skills to enhance student learning and, at the same time, reinforce the more specific language skills taught by reading, writing, and speech teachers. A "writing-across-the curriculum" program, to use the phrase coined by James Britton, places some responsibility for language instruction with every teacher.

We believe that a comprehensive program must start from certain pedagogical premises: (1) that communication education (primarily writing, but including reading, speaking, and listening) is the responsibility of the entire academic community, (2) that such education must be integrated across departmental boundaries, and (3) that it must be continuous during all four years of undergraduate education. Furthermore, a comprehensive language program must incorporate the several roles language plays in education: to communicate, to learn, and to form values. While these roles are not mutually exclusive or exhaustive, we have found it useful to distinguish them in order to better understand and talk about them.

Writing to communicate—or what James Britton calls "transactional writing"—means writing to accomplish something, to inform, instruct, or persuade. This has been the traditional emphasis of most rhetorical texts on expository writing, where audience and purpose define our voice and determine our tone. Communicating information to a particular audience involves all of the writer's skills from invention through revision. Expository writing of all kinds falls into this category: essays, reports, and term papers in school settings; letters, memos, and proposals in work settings.

Writing to learn is different. We write to ourselves as well as talk with others to objectify our perceptions of reality; the primary function of this "expressive" language is not to communicate, but to order and represent experience to our own understanding. In this sense language provides us with a unique way of knowing and becomes a tool for discovering, for shaping meaning, and for reaching understanding. For many writers this kind of speculative writing takes place in notebooks and journals; often it is first-draft writing, necessary before more formal, finished writing can be done.

Finally, writing is a value-forming activity, a means of finding our voice as well as making our voice heard. The act of writing allows authors to distance themselves from experience and helps them to interpret, clarify, and place value on that experience; thus, writers can become spectators using language to further define themselves and their beliefs. This value-forming activity is perhaps the most personally and socially significant role writing plays in our education; this role must not be forgotten or lost as we also attempt to produce careful, clear, and correct prose.

Given that writing has several functions, teachers in all disciplines can provide opportunities for individuals to explore through writing their relationship to knowledge, articulate it, and scrutinize its value. When students begin to understand and appreciate the full potential of written language, their respect for the conventions of writing well increases.

The cross-disciplinary writing program we developed at Michigan Technological University is teacher-centered. This framework assumes —computers and television aside—that the teacher is still the center of educational experience. Other schools have taken different routes to improve writing proficiency for all students: junior-level competency examinations, for example, or senior-level writing courses required of all students. We believe that people soon forget knowledge acquired under an examination approach; we don't believe that one more required course in our students' jam-packed curriculum will make them truly better writers. Our program attempts to achieve more fundamental changes than either of these solutions by addressing the students' total work across the school curriculum.

We conduct off-campus writing workshops to educate teachers from all disciplines in the functions and processes of language and, at the same time, provide assistance with pedagogical strategies so that they, in turn, can teach their students to use language in a variety of meaningful ways. Through the format of these workshops we explore theoretical ideas and consider whether or not they may lead to useful classroom practices. We actively promote certain experience-based premises about teaching writing: that students learn to write by writing and rewriting, that students need to write often to become fluent, and that writing should serve different purposes and audiences to remain interesting and challenging to the writers. In addition to the four-day summer workshops, our particular program involves academic-year seminars on writing for different university departments, follow-up activities for former workshop participants, a newsletter network, a university-wide language skills laboratory, and interdisciplinary re-search by writing and reading teachers.

Like many comprehensive programs we have borrowed ideas freely from colleagues at other places—Beaver College, the University of Michigan, and the National Writing Project, for example—but the primary influence on both our program and our book has been the first-hand experience of conducting interdisciplinary writing work-shops. We have tried as much as possible to incorporate the principles which govern the workshops into this text. All of the authors in this book have participated, in one way or another, in the interdisciplinary writing workshops; all but one are currently teaching in the Michigan Tech Humanities Department.

Randall Freisinger introduces the conceptual framework for writing across the curriculum programs. He asserts that attention to the com-posing process and to inquiry-oriented learning serves the goals of liberal education.

Toby Fulwiler and Carol Berkenkotter explain the uses of expressive writing in learning, idea generation, and problem solving. Fulwiler provides practical suggestions for journal writing in all disciplines, while Berkenkotter suggests ways in which traditional problem-solving models can be applied to composing, particularly to the early stages which often prove especially difficult for student writers.

Robert Jones and Toby Fulwiler discuss strategies for using formal writing in the classroom, including assignments and evaluation. Jack Jobst focuses on the role of audience in writing and delineates the numerous audiences inside and outside the classroom. Both of these chapters focus on "transactional writing," that is, on communicating information.

The next two chapters suggest ways in which poetic and narrative forms enhance learning by providing students with a means of engaging ideas and evaluating experience. Art Young demonstrates how student writers can bring both their imaginations and value systems to bear on the subject matter of a class by writing in various creative forms. James Kalmbach and William Powers discuss particular ways in which the narrative or "story telling" mode provides a perspective on new knowledge.

The reading process is the principal focus for Bruce Petersen, Anne Falke, and Elizabeth Flynn. Petersen demonstrates how the subjective nature of the reading process calls for writing assignments which make knowledge personal. In her overview of recent research on reading, Falke contributes an exposition of how people learn from reading. Flynn discusses developing students' reading abilities in relation to particular subject matters.

Two chapters offer techniques for teachers who work with students orally, individually, or in small writing groups; they attest to the invaluable contribution talking and listening make to the learning process. Peter Schiff provides a variety of methods for conferencing with students and giving feedback on writing assignments. Diana Freisinger and Jill Burkland describe the role of the writing lab tutor in developing student writing abilities and offer useful suggestions to classroom teachers on advising and assisting students with a particular writing assignment.

An annotated bibliography on language and learning across the curriculum, prepared and annotated by Bruce Petersen, concludes our book. It provides a useful starting point for those teachers and educators who wish to further understand the concepts and practices implied by the phrase "writing across the curriculum."

Throughout this book we have tried to provide teachers with a provocative mixture of theoretical ideas and practical classroom activities. No one teacher could or should use all of the ideas presented here; however, we believe that every teacher, regardless of academic specialty, can find something here for speculation if not practice. In order to teach writing well, instructors need neither magic nor rules; instead, they need only to examine and understand the role played by language in learning. We hope this volume contributes toward such an understanding.

Acknowledgments

We would like to thank the people who helped us develop the "writing across the curriculum" program at Michigan Technological University and who helped create this book, which grew out of our work in that program. We appreciate the leadership and support of our university president, Dale F. Stein, who endorsed our efforts from the beginning, and of the General Motors Foundation, whose financial gifts to our university over the past five years made much of our research and program development possible. Special thanks to Lynn Foss and Pat Murphy, who provided necessary typing and secretarial assistance cheerfully and promptly. Thanks also to James Britton for his initial encouragement of this project, Paul O'Dea of NCTE for his guidance, NCTE project editor Philip Heim for crisp editing and good sense, and our students and colleagues, who were willing to participate in our campus-wide experiment. Finally, thanks to Laura, Ann, Megan, Molly, Anna, Sarah, and Kelsey for their good humor and patience.

Toby Fulwiler
Art Young

Language Connections

1 Cross-Disciplinary Writing Programs: Beginnings

Randall Freisinger
Michigan Technological University

A number of high schools and universities in this country are experimenting with writing-across-the-curriculum programs for their faculties. For example, at Michigan Technological University, we have been offering writing workshops since 1977 to explore with faculty from all disciplines how they might use writing more often in their classes. At times these workshops have been controversial because they tap hidden reservoirs of interdisciplinary resentment and frustration. To many of my colleagues outside English, two points seem obvious: the responsibility for teaching students to write belongs exclusively to English teachers, and these teachers have generally failed miserably in meeting this responsibility. (One also senses a growing mistrust of writing teachers whose values and pedagogies transcend the basics.) Writing-across-the-curriculum programs challenge these traditionalist attitudes. To be effective, the workshop staff must know and be sympathetic with the concerns of their colleagues from other fields; they must operate from a solid, carefully researched theoretical foundation which appeals to other disciplines as well as to the humanities.

Writing-across-the-curriculum programs are appearing in reaction against the dominant view of language in schools, namely, that language has only one function—to inform—and that the only language activity useful to education is the finished report or essay. To counter this view, Michigan Tech's writing-across-the-curriculum project builds its cross-disciplinary workshops around these premises: (1) writing promotes learning; (2) writing is a complex developmental process; and (3) the universe of discourse includes a broad range of writing functions and audiences. Although these premises draw from work in rhetoric, reading, and psychology, they have been most strongly influenced by the conclusions of James Britton and his colleagues at the University of London. Their research,[1] published in 1975, constitutes the center of gravity for our project, as this and many of the following chapters will show.

Writing and Learning

Our program assumes that *language for learning is different from language for informing.*[2] Britton acknowledges these different kinds of language use by distinguishing the expressive, transactional, and poetic functions of language. Expressive language, he says, is language close to the self; it reveals as much about the speaker as it does about the topic. It is the language the writer uses first to draft important ideas. Transactional language, on the other hand, is language for an audience. Its primary aim is to convey information clearly to other people; it is the language of newspapers, law courts, and technical reports. It is also the language of schools. The third mode, poetic language, is the language of art. It is used to create verbal objects, and as such it is as much an aesthetic medium for a writer as clay or paint would be for a sculptor or painter. In our program we are mainly concerned with the first two modes.

We begin by examining the contribution expressive writing can make to learning. This exploratory, close-to-the-self language is important because it is the primary means we have of personalizing knowledge. As philosopher/scientist Michael Polanyi claims, all knowledge, if it is to be genuine, must be somehow made personal.[3] The Russian psychologist Lev Vygotsky tells us in *Thought and Language* that the connection between language and thinking is vital and organic. "The relation between thought and word," he maintains, "is a living process; thought is born through words. A word devoid of thought is a dead thing, and a thought unembodied in words remains a shadow."[4] When students are not allowed to work out their ideas *before* they report them to others, they are dealing in "dead things" (moribund words and ideas can be found with distressing ease in almost any batch of student papers). We believe that language must be employed in classrooms as a tool for discovery, an aid to learning, not merely as an instrument for reporting.

In our project, writing is particularly critical to idea formation. We reject the Think/Write model that reduces writing to the status of stenography, of simple transcription of the mind's fully formed concepts. We join with Janet Emig in her assertion that writing "represents a unique mode of learning—not merely valuable, not merely special, but unique."[5] Expressive writing gets students in touch with themselves; informative writing connects them to others. Genuine communication requires an organic interaction between the two functions. If we teachers, regardless of disciplines, expect our students to write well, we must acknowledge both functions of language and provide opportunities in our assignments for students to operate in both spheres.

If we ignore the organic interdependence of the two functions and attend only to the surface structure, to the product, in so doing we encourage the deep structure function of writing to atrophy. When writing is used exclusively to test students or to solicit information from them, we imply (a) that the students are little more than memory banks for *our* information, and (b) that writing is something we do *after* we have learned. A not-so-mad analogy occurs to me here: Our students are like the soldier in white in Joseph Heller's *Catch-22;* we pump the clear fluid of "objective knowledge" into them and judge their success according to how clear the fluid is when it comes back out. As the artillery captain said to Yossarian, "Why can't they hook the two jars up to each other and eliminate the middleman? What the hell do they need him for?"

How widespread is this preference for writing as informing in our schools today? Britton has demonstrated the overwhelming partiality in British schools to transactional writing. Working with a sample of approximately 2,000 student papers drawn from four grade levels across the curriculum, his team reached several conclusions: (1) By far the most dominant of the modes was the transactional, constituting nearly 64 percent of the sample; (2) Poetic writing occurred in about 18 percent of the papers; (3) Expressive writing is found in less than 6 percent of the sample. The farther along in school children go, the less expressive writing they are asked to perform. They are asked to do an increasing amount of transactional writing, most of which requires them to inform rather than to speculate or persuade. Britton sees serious implications in these figures: "The small amount of speculative writing certainly suggests that, for whatever reason, curricular aims did not include the fostering of writing that reflects independent thinking."[6] Students appear to be performing informative writing tasks "without engaging in the thinking processes required to give full meaning to what is learnt."[7]

No comparable study has yet been made of American schools, but Janet Emig found in her research on the composing behavior of twelfth graders that, at least in composition classes, the chief school-sponsored mode is extensive (i.e., transactional). She concludes:

> The teaching of composition at this level is essentially unimodal, with only extensive writing given sanction in many schools. Almost by definition, this mode is other-directed—in fact it is other-centered. The concern is with sending a message, a com-

> munication out into the world for the edification, the enlighten-
> ment, and ultimately the evaluation of another. Too often, the
> other is a teacher, interested chiefly in a product he can criticize
> rather than in a process he can help initiate through imagination
> and sustain through empathy and support.[8]

This reliance on extensive (i.e., transactional) writing in our schools
reflects our educational system's neglect of the discovery function of
language.

The Composing Process

The second of our program premises addresses the failure of our schools
to appreciate the complex, developmental nature of the composing
process. Almost all serious writing tasks, excepting mere copying,
normally involve a process, no matter how implicit and telescoped that
process might be. For mature writers working on a simple writing task,
the process may be mostly unconscious and compressed. But if the
writer's task is complex or if the writer lacks the confidence and fluency
of a mature writer, the process becomes more explicit and protracted.

We approach the composing process from two perspectives. One
focuses on the behavior a writer exhibits in completing a writing task.
Sophisticated work is presently going on in this area.[9] An important
influence on our program has been Janet Emig's *The Composing
Processes of Twelfth Graders.* The most obvious consequence of her
work is that many teachers now give special attention to the writing
process in their classes and are developing strategies to nurture it. This
shift in consciousness from product to process is the single most significant change in composition pedagogy in the last decade.

Our concern with the composing process is even more indebted to
Britton's stress on the relationship between the expressive and transactional modes, particularly his claim that success with the latter grows
out of involvement with the former. Britton says that expressive
language stays close to the speaker or writer and is fully comprehensible only to someone who shares the context—that is, the speaker's
or writer's experience, attitudes, and assumptions. Expressive language
is "utterance at its most relaxed and intimate, as free as possible from
outside demands, whether those of a task or of an audience."[10] Because
it usually serves the unfettered flow of ideas and feelings, expressive
language is the matrix of language use. In other words, transactional
or poetic writing processes should begin in an expressive phase, then
move either toward full, explicit communication for an audience
outside the writer's context (transactional) or toward perfection of a
verbal object (poetic). The closer the writer comes to either objective,

the closer the writer is to the finished product. But the journey (i.e., the process) should begin with an expressive phase.

Why? The answer lies in Britton's view of the composing process, a view which is, admittedly, in conflict with more recent and empirically-based theories of composing behavior, but which, despite its over-simplification, serves to illustrate the important contribution of expressive writing to the final product. Britton divides the process into three stages: conception, incubation, and production. Once the writer knows *that* writing must be done, *what* is expected, and *how* to proceed, the conception stage is completed. It is at this point—while the project incubates—that expressive language, both oral and written, plays a major role. Two factors now exert considerable influence: the writer's desire to get the facts straight and the need to get the information "right with the self." "An essential part of the writing process is," Britton claims, "explaining the matter to oneself."[11] Without this stage, he concludes, "all the careful note-making and selection and arrangement of data can do very little."[12]

The production stage, the actual committing of ideas to paper for an audience, cannot occur in any meaningful way unless the writer has first understood the task that has been given and why the materials are being assembled. Britton concludes that "in the emergence of any original thinking (including under 'original' ideas which are new to the writer but may be familiar to the teacher-reader) there is an expressive stage in that thinking whether the writing is ultimately informative, poetic, or persuasive. It is what the writer makes of these expressive beginnings that determines his thought processes as the written text is produced."[13] These expressive beginnings include classroom talk, interpretive note-taking, journal writing about the problems the writing task has posed, and early drafts. Expressive writing and talking are most useful to the writer as exploratory tools at the beginning of a demanding writing task. The writer works outward from an expressive phase toward transactional writing, the terminal point of a complex, messy process. If this expressive phase is as yet empirically undocumented, it remains as real for writers as the unconscious before Freud, natural selection before Darwin, and the benzene ring before Kekulé.

This, then, is the problem: All too often teachers across the curriculum have limited their conception of language to the communicative or transactional function, thereby ignoring a significant part of the composing process, as well as the contribution of the expressive function to both learning and the final written product. The first two premises upon which cross-disciplinary programs might be founded attempt to solve this problem by demonstrating the learning function of language and by illustrating the role of expressive writing in the composing process.

Our second perspective on the composing process focuses on the developmental nature of writing ability. Long-term acquisition of writing ability depends to a great extent on cognitive growth. This is an especially important point for elementary and secondary teachers, but college teachers should also have some sense of the longitudinal process by which a writer acquires fluency in a language from childhood to early adulthood. James Moffett and James Britton both adopt this sequential approach, and both are influenced by the writings of Jean Piaget, who posits that all humans pass through a series of discrete intellectual stages on their way to cognitive maturity. Piaget outlines four stages of cognitive development: (1) sensorimotor period —birth to two years, (2) preoperational period—two to seven years, (3) concrete operations—seven to eleven years, and (4) formal operations—eleven years through adolescence. The basic direction of this sequence is from physical interaction with the material world to abstract hypotheses about that world, the latter occurring with any sophistication only in the final stage.[14]

High school and college teachers need to be particularly concerned with the transition from concrete operations to formal operations because this last stage represents the flowering of mature, logical thought, and it is the final destination of the education process. At this fourth stage the child acquires the capability to reason, to formulate hypotheses, to deduce, to solve problems and make meanings in the abstract, without dependence on physical manipulation of concrete objects. The adolescent must make this transition in order to perform meaningfully the intellectual tasks expected at the late secondary and college levels. It makes excellent sense, of course, for teachers at those levels to design courses which make demands consonant with the cognitive stage of their students.

In the last ten years, we have seen evidence that as many as half of our students from junior high on into adulthood are apparently unable to think abstractly or to process and produce logical propositions.[15] Many of us know the frustration caused by our students' difficulty in making the transition from summarizing to synthesizing, from retelling to drawing original conclusions. Students seem to lack the ability to find meaning and make structure once they are cut off from chronology. Teachers in other disciplines report comparable experiences. In workshops with biology and social sciences faculty, Michigan Tech's staff has heard the same complaint over and over: the most serious problem in student papers is an inability to think critically, to synthesize, to structure logically.

Excessive reliance on the transactional function of language may be substantially responsible for our students' inability to think critically and independently. We know that if students are provided regular opportunities to work in the expressive mode with new and challenging subject matter, they can improve their critical abilities significantly. In fact, researchers in the sciences have found that a pedagogy which encourages exploration and personal inquiry is more effective than the traditional lecture/product environment in helping students achieve the stage of formal operations.[16]

In the inquiry method, the expressive function of language assumes a crucial role. The goal of this method, quite compatible with Piaget's view of the learning process, is to allow students to expand their image of the world—their "cognitive structure"—by connecting their existing picture to new experiences. As they encounter new materials, they must either assimilate the materials into their image or they must accommodate them—that is, restructure their image to make it compatible with the new information. The key point is this: *These connections must be personal.* They can occur meaningfully in no other way. Expressive language, both oral and written, promotes open-ended exploration of new experiences. Product-oriented, transactional language promotes closure. Its function is to report mastered fact, not to assist learning.

Exploration with expressive language of new materials allows students to achieve what Britton calls "getting it right with the self." Students are afforded the chance to move from confusion to clarity. Such opportunities for personal grasp of new material will, we believe, facilitate the transition from concrete to formal operations. Moreover, students will write more confident, more logical, and more conceptually sophisticated transactional papers.

Our treatment of the composing process is, then, two-dimensional. We seek to demonstrate the importance of expressive language to a single writing task, believing that students must get new subject matter "right with the self" before they attempt to report or argue their conclusions in public discourse. At the same time we see crucial developmental implications underlying the regular practice of expressive writing.

The Universe of Discourse

The third theoretical premise of our writing-across-the-curriculum program is that the universe of discourse includes a much broader range of writing functions and audiences than is normally recognized by teachers. We introduce this concept fairly early in our writing workshops. Our perspective on this premise has been shaped by two major figures: James Moffett and, once again, Britton.[17]

In *Teaching the Universe of Discourse* Moffett classifies writing into four modes, each mode providing the writer with a different point of view: What is happening (drama); What happened (narration); What happens (exposition); and What should happen (argumentation). Moffett believes that writers should have experience in all four modes. These may be taken up sequentially, in order to encourage the writer to decenter, that is, to move from personal to more impersonal forms of discourse. The good writer, Moffett believes, is able to use the stylistic conventions that each mode dictates and write for a variety of audiences.

The coordinates of Moffett's universe of discourse are (a) distance between writer and audience and (b) level of abstraction at which a writer must operate. In each case there is a spectrum. A writer may, at one extreme, be synonymous with the audience (Britton's expressive writing); at the other extreme the writer may be very remote from the audience (writing for publication to a broad and diverse readership). There are, of course, intermediate kinds of audience-distance relationships. Similarly, a writer may operate at different levels of abstraction, each of which makes different cognitive demands on that writer. To record impressions is different from reporting events; reporting an event differs from generalizing about human and historical tendencies; and all of these differ from theorizing about past or future events. Moffett argues that to develop cognitively and stylistically a writer must have repeated experience in both audience shifts and changes in level of abstraction. Exposure to (and practice with) the full universe of discourse enables a writer to acquire rhetorical versatility.

Britton's work bears strong resemblance to Moffett's, though it divides the universe of discourse differently—into expressive, poetic, and transactional modes. Like Moffett, Britton argues for more student opportunities to write in all three modes, but he emphasizes the expressive because it is in that mode that students have the chance to discover what they think before they try to convey their ideas to others. Britton shares Moffett's concern for the role which experience at different levels of abstraction plays in a writer's development. He, too, sees a developmental sequence in the transactional mode: record, report, generalized narrative, low-level analogic, analogic, speculative, tautologic, and conative (persuasive). He believes that developing writers should progress through the sequence of levels of abstraction, not work just at the informative level.

Britton also shares Moffett's concern for the relationship between writer and audience. In *The Development of Writing Abilities (11–18)* Britton claims a crucial role for audience awareness:

> We want to suggest that one important dimension of development
> in writing ability is the growth of a sense of audience, the growth

> of the ability to make adjustments and choices in writing which
> take account of the audience for whom the writing is intended. . . .
> A highly developed sense of audience must be one of the marks of
> the competent mature writer.[18]

Working with a sample of student papers, Britton and his team wanted
to determine whether or not young writers were actually being asked
to write for a variety of audiences in order to develop confidence and
flexibility in a number of "voices." The main audience categories that
the research team identified were self, teacher, wider audience (known),
and unknown audience. Within the teacher category there are these
sub-categories: child (or adolescent) to trusted adult, pupil to teacher
(general), pupil to teacher (particular relationship), and pupil to
examiner.[19] The basic results of Britton's study are both revealing and
disturbing. (1) The amount of writing to oneself as audience (expressive
writing) was negligible, constituting only 0.5 percent. (2) The highest
percentage of writing—nearly 95 percent—fell within the teacher category, most of it to teacher as examiner or teacher (general). (3) In
subjects other than English and Religious Education, the percentage of
teacher-as-examiner writing was very high (History, 69 percent; Geography, 81 percent; Science, 87 percent). There was, in other words,
across the curriculum, little variety in audience.

Britton's hypothesis is that such a narrow range of audience options
inhibits the development of student writers, particularly their ability
to adapt style and content to a large and unknown audience, the most
difficult and mature form of discourse. Britton's findings regarding
writing function and audience are ultimately intertwined. As he ob-
serves, "It would appear . . . that the pressures to write at an analogic
level of the informative—and in the main for an audience of the teacher
as examiner—were great enough both to inhibit early expressive writing and to prevent any but minimal development into the more abstract
levels of the informative."[20]

It follows that teachers in all disciplines should increase student
opportunities for expressive writing and expand the range of target
audiences for which they have their students write. These changes must
not be left exclusively to English teachers, nor are these changes the
responsibility only of elementary and secondary staffs. The development of writing ability is the responsibility of *all teachers* in *all disciplines* at *all educational levels.*

When we talk of the problem of literacy, we are speaking of a
problem whose boundaries remain as yet uncharted and whose causes
are controversial and elusive. But, despite the difficulties, we must
make a beginning. Sweeping educational reforms may be required in
curriculum design and teacher training. Yet we need not wait for such
reforms in order to begin what amounts, metaphorically, to reclama-

tion or urban renewal. If we teachers, at all levels and in all disciplines, will use language to promote learning as well as informing; if we will approach writing as a complex developmental process; and if we will encourage students to travel extensively in the universe of discourse, then we can become both enablers and ennoblers, and we can help students discover the power of language to which, naturally or not, they are heirs.

Notes

1. James Britton, Tony Burgess, Nancy Martin, Alex McLeod, and Harold Rosen, *The Development of Writing Abilities (11–18)* (London: Macmillan Education, 1975).

2. Some pairs of distinctions that parallel this formulation of the dual function of language appear regularly in the literature of language theory. See for example Janet Emig's reflexive and extensive modes in *The Composing Processes of Twelfth Graders* (Champaign, Ill.: NCTE, 1971); James Moffett's I-It and I-You language in *Teaching the Universe of Discourse* (Boston: Houghton Mifflin, 1968); Linda S. Flower's and John R. Hayes' writer-based and reader-based prose in "Problem Solving Strategies and the Writing Process," *College English* 39 (December 1977): 449–461; Martin Nystrand's heuristic and explicative language processes in "Language as Discovery and Exploration: Heuristic and Explicative Uses of Language," *Language as a Way of Knowing*, ed. Martin Nystrand (Toronto: The Ontario Institute for Studies in Education, 1977).

3. *Personal Knowledge* (London: Routledge and Kegan Paul, 1958).

4. Trans E. Haufmann and G. Vakar (Cambridge, Mass.: The MIT Press, 1962), p. 153.

5. Emig, "Writing as a Mode of Learning," *College Composition and Communication* 28 (May 1977): 122-127.

6. Britton, p. 197.

7. Britton, p. 198.

8. *The Composing Processes of Twelfth Graders* (Urbana, Ill.: NCTE, 1971) p. 97.

9. E.g., Sondra Perl's research and that of Linda Flower and John Hayes. For a summary of research on the composing process see Emig's review of the literature in *The Composing Processes of Twelfth Graders*, pp. 7-28.

10. Britton, p. 82.

11. Britton, p. 28.

12. Britton, p. 29.

13. Britton, pp. 30-31.

14. For a more complete explanation see J. Piaget and B. Inhelder, *The Psychology of One Child* (New York: Basic Books, 1969).

15. See Arnold B. Arons and Robert Karplus, "Implications of Accumulating Data on Levels of Intellectual Development," *American Journal of Physics* 44 (April 1976): 396; Elaine Cohen and David A. Smith-Gold, "Your

Students' Cognitive Functioning: An Important Factor in Readiness to Learn," *Proceedings of the Eleventh Annual Conference of the Western College Reading Association* 11 (March 1978): 31–34; Joe W. McKinnon and John W. Renner, "Are Colleges Concerned with Intellectual Development?" *American Journal of Physics* 39 (September 1971): 1047–1052.

16. See for examples John W. Renner and Anton E. Lawson, "Piagetian Theory and Instruction in Physics," *Physics Teacher* 11 (March 1973): 165–169; Renner and Lawson, "Promoting Intellectual Development through Science Teaching," *Physics Teacher* 11 (May 1973): 273–276; David P. Ausubel, "The Transition from Concrete to Abstract Functioning: Theoretical Issues and Implications for Education," *Journal of Research in Science Teaching* 2 (1964): 261–266. A good working bibliography can be found at the conclusion of Anton Lawson and Warren Wollman, "Encouraging the Transition from Concrete to Formal Cognitive Functioning—An Experiment," *Journal of Research in Science Teaching* 13 (1976): 413–430.

17. A third book which has influenced our project's concern for a broader view of writing is James Kinneavy's *A Theory of Discourse* (Englewood Cliffs, N.J.: Prentice-Hall, 1971). Using the communications triangle as a starting point, Kinneavy finds implicit in it four kinds of discourse: expressive, referential, literary, and persuasive. There are obvious parallels here to Britton and Moffett. All three writers demonstrate the variety of functions and audiences which writing serves, and they encourage development of assignments which require students to write in different modes and for different audiences.

18. Britton, p. 58.

19. For additional sub-categories, see Britton, p. 66. Detailed explanations of each of these audiences are found in pp. 66–73.

20. Britton, p. 197.

2 The Personal Connection: Journal Writing across the Curriculum

Toby Fulwiler
Michigan Technological University

> The part that was said about writing stuff down in your own words to clarify or remember something, I really agree with. Even when I copy over a batch of notes or something, I remember it a lot better. . . . I've heard a few people say that by keeping a journal, their writing abilities increased. This could help me. (Bruce M.)

Teachers sometimes look suspiciously at journal writing. For some it is too personal, unstructured or informal to assign in the classroom; for others it is too difficult to measure; and for still others journal writing simply serves no practical pedagogical purpose—it is a waste of time. The premise of this chapter, however, is that the journal can be both a formal rigorous assignment and, at the same time, a place for students to practice imaginative and speculative thinking. Journal writing, in the broadest sense, is an interdisciplinary learning tool with a place in every academic classroom[1]; it is not the sole province of the English teacher any more than numbers belong to the math teacher, or speaking belongs to the speech teacher.

A dozen years ago, when I began teaching college English, I sometimes assigned journals in composition and literature classes but used them sparingly in the classroom itself, preferring to let students write on their own. Some students used them well, while most never really understood what kind of writing they were supposed to do in them. I no longer trust to chance. Journals "work" now for most students in my classes because we use them actively, every day to write in, read from, and talk about—in addition to whatever private writing the students do on their own. These everyday journal writes take the place of other routine writing assignments from pop quizzes to book reports. Journal writing in class stimulates student discussion, starts small group activity, clarifies hazy issues, reinforces learning experience, and stimulates student imagination.

15

Journal writing works because every time a person writes an entry, instruction is individualized; the act of silent writing, even for five minutes, generates ideas, observations, emotions. It is hard to day-dream, doze off, or fidget while one writes—unless one writes about it. I don't believe that journal writing will make passive students miracu-lously active learners; however, such writing makes it harder for stu-dents to remain passive.

At Michigan Technological University we conduct off-campus writing workshops to introduce our colleagues to a variety of ideas for using writing to enhance both learning and communication skills. Workshop topics include: (1) invention and brainstorming, (2) re-writing and revision, (3) editing, (4) peer-response groups, (5) evalua-tion, and (6) journal writing. In these interdisciplinary workshops we ask teachers of history, chemistry, and business to keep journals, themselves, for the duration of the workshop. Sometimes we start a session by asking the participants to write down their opinion about the causes of poor student writing. Other times we ask the teachers to summarize or evaluate the worth of a particular workshop—on revision or editing, for example—by writing about it for five minutes in their journals. And still other times we ask them to "free write" in order to generate possible paper topics which will be expanded, later, into short papers. These five and ten-minute writing exercises allow teachers to experience first-hand the potential of journal writing as an aid to learning.

Teachers in all subject areas and all grade levels find it easy to add more writing to a class by using journals. Regardless of class size, this kind of informal writing need not take more teacher time. Journals can be spot checked, skimmed, read thoroughly, or not read at all, depending on the teacher's interest and purpose. Journals have proved to be remarkably flexible documents; some teachers call them "logs," others "commonplace books," still others "writers' notebooks." While I prefer students to keep looseleaf binders, science teachers who are conscious of patent rights often require bound notebooks. While I suggest pens (pencils smear), a forestry teacher suggests pencils (ink smears in the rain). And so on.

Student Academic Journals

What does a journal look like? How often should people write in them? What kinds of writing should they do on their own? How should I grade them? These questions often occur to the teacher who has not used or kept journals before. Following are some possible answers.

Journals might be looked at as part of a continuum including diaries and class notebooks: while diaries record the private thought and experience of the writer, class notebooks record the public thought and presentation of the teacher. The journal is somewhere between the two. Like the diary, the journal is written in the first person about ideas important to the writer; like the class notebook, the journal may focus on academic subjects the writer wishes to examine.

Diary	Journal	Class Notebook
(Subjective Expression)	(I/It)	(Objective Topics)

Journals may be focused narrowly, on the subject matter of one discipline, or broadly, on the whole range of a person's experience. Each journal entry is a deliberate exercise in expansion: "How far can I take this idea? How accurately can I describe or explain it? How can I make it make sense to me?" The journal encourages writers to become conscious, through language, of what is happening to them, both personally and academically.

Student writers should be encouraged to experiment with their journals, to write often and regularly on a wide variety of topics, to take some risks with form, style, and voice. Students should notice how writing in the early morning differs from writing late at night. They might also experience how writing at the same time every day, regardless of inclination or mood, often produces surprising results. Dorothy Lambert relaxes students by suggesting that "a journal is a place to fail. That is, a place to try, experiment, test one's wings. For the moment, judgment, criticism, evaluation are suspended; what matters is the attempt, not the success of the attempt."[2] She asks students to pay attention to writing as a process and quit worrying about product perfection—in this case, correct spelling, grammar, punctuation, form, diction, and style. For better or worse, the journal is the student's own voice; the student must know this and the teacher respect it.

Peter Elbow urges students to explore and discover through "free writing," a technique that encourages writers to free associate while writing as fast as they can. Elbow writes: "You don't have to think hard or prepare or be in the mood: without stopping, just write whatever words come out—whether or not you are thinking or in the mood."[3] This process illustrates immediately, for most writers, the close relationship between writing and thinking. The journal is a natural place to write freely. Students can practice it on their own to get their mental gears moving toward a paper topic; teachers can assign such uninhibited writing to brainstorm new research projects. Keeping these exercises in journals guarantees a written record of the ideas generated, which may prove useful during the term of study or, later, to document intellectual growth.

The significance of journals as records of thought cannot be under-estimated by teachers who value independent thinking. The journal records the student's individual travel through the academic world; at the same time it serves well when formal papers or projects need to be written. Ken Macrorie calls journals the "seedbeds" from which other, more public (transactional or poetic) kinds of writing will emerge.[4] Echoing Macrorie, Mark Hanson advocates using personal journals "to generate (both) academic and creative writings"; journal entries are the primary "sources" for educational growth, regardless of subject area.[5] Field notes jotted in a biology notebook become an extended observation written in a "biology journal"; this entry, in turn, might well become the basis for a major research project. Personal reflections recorded in a history journal can help the student identify with, and perhaps make sense of, the otherwise distant and confusing past. Trial hypotheses might find first articulation in social science journals; the strongest idea will provide the impetus for further experimentation and study.

Journal Assignments

Starting class. Introduce a class with a five-minute journal write. Any class. Any subject. Use the journal to bridge the gap between the student's former activity (walking, talking, eating, listening) and your classroom. In a discussion class, suggest a topic related to the day's lesson—a quote from the reading assignment, for instance—and allow those first few minutes for students to compose (literally) their thoughts and focus them in a public direction; without that time, the initial discussion is often halting and groping. After such a journal entry, the teacher may ask someone to read an entry out loud to start people talking. It is hard sometimes to read rapidly written words in public, but it is also rewarding when the language generates a response from classmates. I often read my own entry first to put the students at ease, for my sentences may be awkward, halting, and fragmentary just as theirs sometimes are. Repeated periodically, this exercise provides students with a structured oral entry into the difficult public arena of the classroom and helps affirm the value of their personal voice.

Like the discussion class, the lecture also benefits from a transition exercise which starts students thinking about the scheduled topic. For example, prior to beginning a lecture in a nineteenth-century American literature class studying "Transcendentalism," I might ask students to define their concept of "romanticism" in their journals. I might then commence lecturing directly, using the brief writing time to set the scene or mood for the lecture; or I might start a short discussion based on the student writing as a lead into the lecture. Either way, the students involve themselves with the material because they have committed themselves, through their own language, to at least a tentative exploration of an idea.

Summarizing. End a class with a journal write. This exercise asks students to pull together, in summary fashion, information or ideas they have learned during class. The summary serves several purposes: "What did you learn in here today—one thing—anything?" or "What questions are still unanswered?" These issues can be handled orally, of course, without recourse to the journal, but forcing loose thoughts onto paper often generates tighter thinking. Too often instructors lecture right up to the bell, still trying to make one last point. Better, perhaps, to cover less lecture territory and to end the class with students' own observations and summary in journals. That final act of writing/thinking helps students synthesize material for themselves, and so increases its value.

In the following journal entry, written at the end of the first day in a humanities class, a student writes his way toward an answer to the question "What are the humanities?"[6]

A definition of humanities? Kind of a tough question. I really didn't have any idea before the class discussion today. I could've guessed that it had something to do with humans just looking at the word. A dictionary definition probably wouldn't help either. They never do. So, I guess, by remembering what was said I'll have to think of something myself. At first I thought about just human behavior but when I think of humanities I think of English and that doesn't fit in. It seems that human creative expression or communication would be a good, short definition. Because I consider photography, drawing, painting, writing, building, and lots of other stuff to be creative human expression. Humanities has to be a very general topic; so the definition would also have to be general. When someone mentioned subjective, I agreed with that a lot. I think that separates it pretty well with the sciences. Scientists all seem to be very objective people with objective purposes. They have to make precise decisions and don't really seem to have any feelings toward what they do. I mean, they may get involved in the things they do, but while they're working they don't seem to get emotional about it or anything. So, I think if you said the humanities are human creative expressions, it would include a lot of things that most people think of when they hear the word.

This entry is typical of a person using his writing to think with. He repeats the questions, reflects on his prior knowledge, digresses about dictionaries, thinks about class discussion, tries a sample definition, expands and narrows his conceptions, compares and contrasts, and finally arrives at a definition which satisfies him for the time being. What we see in the form of a product (the journal passage itself) is actually most valuable to the student as a process (what went on in the student's head while writing). Phrases like "I guess," "I think," "It seems," "I mean"—some repeated several times in this text—indicate attempts to make sense of the teacher's question through the student's own language. Other trigger words in this passage are past-tense constructions ("I agreed" and "I thought") which reveal the writer testing prior assumptions against both the definition question and what went on in class that day.

This passage is a summary journal write; at the same time it is typical of the thinking process which journal writing in general encourages. The digressions, dead-ends, awkward constructions, and repetitions typify our thinking process when we are trying to solve a new problem or come to grips with a new idea. The student tries to make the problem "personal"; whatever new definition he arrives at will have to be tested against personal experience with the humanities ("photography, drawing, painting, writing, building") on the one hand and his experience with scientists ("very objective people with objective purposes") on the other. This ten-minute activity at the end of a class period has called forth from the student a variety of learning strategies to help him synthesize important issues talked about during class.

Focusing. Interrupt a class lecture with a journal write. Listening is passive and note-taking often mechanical; even the best students drift into daydreams from time to time. Writing changes the pace of the class; it shifts the learners into a participant role. Writing clears out a little space for students to interact with the ideas thrown at them and allows them to focus problems while the stimulus is still fresh.

A professor of American history at Michigan Tech used journals as a regular part of his course in "Michigan History." In discussing the railroad system of the state, for example, he asked students to write for five minutes about their current knowledge of trains—from personal experience, movies, or books. This brief writing time engaged his students more personally with the topic of his lecture. Later in the term, he based exam questions on the midterm and final on some of the inclass journal writing.

A variation on the planned lecture pause is the spontaneous pause, where the lecturer senses misunderstanding in the audience or where the lecturer loses track of an idea. While writing in journals, either teachers or students may put their finger on the problem and so make the next fifteen or twenty minutes more profitable. Of course, instructors do not plan for misunderstanding, but if it occurs, journal writing is one way out.

A digressive or rambling discussion may be refocused by simply calling "Time out" and asking students to write for a few minutes in their journals: "What are we trying to explain?" or "Restate the argument in your own words; then let's start again." In one-sided discussions, where a few students dominate and others can't particpate, interrupt with a short writing task and sometimes the situation reverses itself, as the quiet ones find their voices while the loud ones cool off. The group also can become more conscious of the roles people play in class by asking questions like: "What is your part in this discussion?" or "Try to trace how we got from molecules to psychopaths in the last fifteen minutes" or "Why do you think Tom just said what he did?" Writing about talking provides distance and helps to generate thoughts we didn't have before.

Problem solving. Use journals as a vehicle for posing and solving problems. In a class on modern literature ask students to write about the lines in an e. e. cummings poem which they do not understand; the following day many students will have written their way to understanding by forcing their confusion into sentences. What better way to make sense out of "what if a much of a which of a wind" or "my father moved through dooms of love"? Math or science teachers might ask their students to solve difficult equations by using journal writing when they are confused. For example, Margaret Watson, a high school teacher from Duncan, Oklahoma, reports that using journals in her mathematics classes has improved her students' ability to solve math problems.[7] She asks students questions such as: "The problem I had completing a square was . . ." and "This is how to. . . ." Watson reads the journals and comments to each student individually about his or her feelings about mathematics. Watson writes: "This two-way conversation has been beneficial to the class. The students realize I hear them and care. They seem to have looked inside themselves and to have seen what they could do to help solve their mathematical problems. Many of their grades improved."

The journal could become a regular tool in any subject area to assist students in solving problems, since the act of writing out the problem is, itself, a clarifying experience. Switching from number symbols to word symbols sometimes makes a difference; putting someone else's problem into your own language makes it *your* problem and so leads you one step further toward solution. The key, in other words, is articulating to yourself what the problem is and what you might do about it. Following is a brief example of a student talking to himself about a writing block:

> I'm making this report a hell of a lot harder than it should be. I think my problem is I try to edit as I write. I think what I need to do is first get a basic outline of what I want to write then just write whatever I want. After I'm through, then edit and organize. It's hard for me though.

Homework. Assign journal writing for students to do outside of class. Suggest that students respond to questions or ideas that were highlighted in the day's class or ask questions which would prepare them better for the next class. Teachers might ask students to keep a written journal record of their responses to a current issue; on a given day these responses would form the basis for a more formal class discussion. By using the journal as the place to record students go one step beyond thinking vaguely about their responses but stay short of a formal written assignment which might cause unproductive anxiety over form or style. In some disciplines, like engineering, math, or physics, homework questions might be less "open-ended" than ones asked in liberal arts courses, but even in the most specialized fields some free, imaginative speculation helps. When that speculation is recorded in the journal, students have a record to look at, later, to show where they've been and perhaps suggest where to go next.

Science and social science teachers might ask students to keep a "lab journal" in addition to a lab notebook to record thoughts about their experiments. This adds a personal dimension to keeping records and also provides a place to make connections between one observation and the next. Journal entries could be interleafed next to the recorded data. The same may be done with a "field notebook" in biology or forestry: to the objective data add each student's own thoughts about that data. Such personal observations might prove useful in writing a report or suggest the germ for another paper or project.

A Michigan Tech political science professor uses journals for a variety of homework assignments in his course on "American Government and Politics." He asks students to record frequently their opinions about current events. He also asks students to write short personal summaries of articles in their journals, thereby creating a sequential critical record of course readings. While both of these activities may be conducted through other written forms, using the journal is simple and economical for both students and teacher.

A teacher of music at Michigan Tech asked her students for a term to keep "listening journals," in which to record their daily experience of hearing music. Periodically, she conducted discussion classes which relied heavily on the subjective content of the journals, and so involved the students both personally and critically in her course content. In similar fashion, a Michigan Tech drama teacher currently asks his actors to keep a journal to develop more fully their awareness of a character or scene in a play. He has found that his student actors can write their way into their characters by using journals.

Progress reports. Use journals to monitor student progress through the class. One Michigan Tech metallurgy professor has prepared a full-page handout with suggestions to students about using journals to encourage thoughtful reflection upon important topics, to practice writing answers to possible exam questions, and to improve writing fluency. More specifically, he asks students to write about each day's lecture topic prior to attending class; after class, they are asked to write a class summary or write out questions about the lecture. Periodically, these journals are checked to monitor student progress through the course; they are not graded.

This professor also monitored his own teaching through the journals. In reading his first batch of one hundred journals he was surprised to find so few charts, diagrams, or drawings. As a consequence, he introduced a section on "visual thinking" into his course, as he believes that metallurgical engineers must develop visualization skills to a high degree.

A geography professor at Michigan Tech has used journals for ten years in large lecture classes.[8] In "Recreational Geography" he asks students to keep journals to stimulate their powers of observation. Because they must record their observations, the students look more closely and carefully and, hence, begin to acquire the rudimentary techniques of scientific observation. He also requires students in "Conservation" to keep journals; specifically, at the beginning of new course topics, he asks them to write definitions of terms or concepts which they misuse or misunderstand. At the conclusion of each topic he requests another written definition for comparison with their initial perceptions. During the final week of the ten-week course he asks students to compose an essay about how the course changed their attitude toward conservation. The journal is the primary resource for this last assignment, revealing to both instructor and student what has been learned, what not.

I often ask students to make informal progress reports to themselves about what they are learning in my class. I'm interested in having students share these thoughts with me and/or the class. I often ask for volunteers to read passages out loud after such an assignment. But more important, I think, are the observations students make to themselves about what they are learning. My question is the catalyst, but the insights are only of real value if they are self-initiated. Following is a sample response from a student studying technical writing; it refers to an exercise in which the entire class "agreed" that one piece of writing was better than another:

> After, we took a vote and decided which proposal letter we liked the best—it really made me wonder. I hadn't realized it but we've been conditioned to look for certain things in this class. I guess that's the purpose of any class, strange how you don't notice it happening though.

Class texts. Ask students to write to each other, informally, about concerns and questions raised in the class. By reading passages out loud, or reproducing passages to share with the class, students become more conscious of how their language affects people. Students in my first year humanities class actually suggested that duplicated journal passages should become a part of the "humanistic" content of the course; we mimeographed selected journal entries, shared them for a week and all learned more about each other. Passing these journal writes around class suggested new writing possibilities to the students. In this case, the stimulus to experiment came from classmates rather than the teacher and so had the strong validity of peer education.

An entry such as the following, written about a geography class, can go a long way toward provoking classmates into a discussion of topical issues:

> I don't know if I'm just over-reacting to my Conservation class or not, but lately I've become suspicious of the air, water, and food around me. First we're taught about water polluton, and I find out that the Portage Canal merrily flowing right in front of my house is unfit for human contact because of the sewage treatment plant and how it overflows with every hard rain. Worse yet, I'm told raw sewage flows next to Bridge Street. I used to admire Douglas Houghton Falls for its natural beauty, now all I think of is, "That's raw untreated sewage flowing there."
>
> Our next topic was air pollution. Today I was informed that the rain here in the U.P. has acid levels ten times what it should, thanks to sulfur oxide pollution originating in Minneapolis and Duluth. I'm quite familiar back home in Ishpeming with orange birch trees due to iron ore pelletizing plants.
>
> Is there any escaping this all encompassing wave of pollution? I had thought the Copper Country was a refuge from the poisonous fact of pollution, but I guess its not just Detroit's problem anymore. As I write these words, in countless places around the globe, old Mother Nature is being raped in the foulest way. I get the feeling someday she'll retaliate and we'll deserve it. Every bit of it.

Personal Journals

I am not concerned with *what* students write in their journals, nor even if they respond to all my suggestions. One student, for example, felt she wasn't doing the journal writes "correctly" in my nineteenth-century American literature class because she kept drifting off into personal reflections and writing about her own religious convictions instead of role-playing an imaginary Harvard divinity student responding to Emerson, as I had requested. What could I say? She made the material her own in the most useful way possible. I suspect that the best journal writes deviate far and freely from the questions I pose —and that's fine.

A student's journal can be a documentary of personal as well as academic growth, a record of evolving insight as well as the tool to gain that insight. In classes which explore values, such as philosophy, sociology, and literature, the journal can be a vehicle to explore the writer's own belief system.[9] In like manner, writing classes may benefit from using the journal as a vehicle for self-discovery. In *On Righting Writing*, Robert Rennert reports using a journal for deliberate values-clarification purposes throughout the semester.[10] He asks students to use journals to rank their values, to make lists of "important human qualities," and to write their own "obituaries." He confronts students and makes them objectify, to some extent, their own biases through responses to topics such as "What I want my clothes to say about me." Rennert reports encouraging results from his journal-focused class: "Confronted with significant questions and problems, students moved off dead center and were stimulated to discover, through writing, knowledge about their values and attitudes."

In *Composition for Personal Growth*, Hawley, Simon, and Britton offer teachers suggestions for posing developmental problems for their students. Under the heading "Journal—Synthesizing Activities," Hawley lists a number of imaginary situations which require journal writers to move outside their writing and experience it from a different perspective. In an exercise called "Time Capsule" students are given these directions: "Your journal is discovered one hundred years from now (or three hundred years ago). You, your other-time counterpart, find the journal. Write a description of the person and the way of life revealed in the journal."[11] Tasks such as these provide students with the means to witness their own progress and, as such, are useful concluding exercises in any class using journals.

The journal is a natural format for self-examination. The teacher can initiate the process by suggesting journal writes on traditional value-clarification questions: If your house was on fire and you could only save one object, what would it be? If you had only two more days to live, how would you spend them? Sometimes I pose a general question to a class, at the end of the term, and ask students which particular entries have been most valuable for them to write. This causes some useful review and helps students clarify the journal writing assignments for themselves. Following is a brief example from a class in technical writing:

> Not to be trite or anything—I don't know if that's even the right word. The first entry was the one that helped me the most. It got me started at writing in a journal—in this journal. My sanity has been saved. I can't keep all my problems locked up inside me but I hate telling others—burdening them with my problems. The hardest thing to do is to start something—so my first entry was the hardest. The rest has been easy—somewhat. My professor is the only one who's ever made me have a journal. I was afraid I couldn't do it cuz I never have been able to keep a good diary.

More important, perhaps, than personal journal entries assigned by teachers are the personal entries initiated by students about topics close to themselves. Sometimes students volunteer to show me their more personal sections—I never request them—and it is then that I am convinced that the personal entries will remain, for most students, their most important writing. Sometimes I find students generating (or recording?) strong personal insights, such as the following:

> I think I should quit complaining about being misunderstood . . . since I don't try very hard to be understandable, it's no wonder people don't. I just get ticked because more people don't even seem to *try* to understand others. So many people talk, instead of listening. (I think I'm scared of the ones who listen.)

Personal journals are *not* the business of the classroom teacher. However, it is obvious that what students write to themselves, about themselves, as they journey through the academic curriculum has a lot to do with "education." We cannot and should not monitor these personal trips, but we should, perhaps acknowledge them and encourage students to chronicle them wherever and whenever they can. Again, the journal is one vehicle for such journeys.

Teacher Journals

Teachers who have not done so should try keeping a journal along with their students. Journals do not work for everyone; however, the experience of keeping one may be the only way to find out. Teachers, especially, can profit by the regular introspection and self-examination forced by the process of journal writing. The journal allows sequential planning within the context of one's course—its pages become a record of what has worked, what hasn't, and suggestions for what might work next time—either next class or next year. Teachers can use journals for lesson plans, to work out practice exercises, and to conduct an ongoing class evaluation. The journal may become a teaching workshop and a catalyst for new research ideas as well as a record of pedagogical growth.

Teachers should consider doing journal writing daily, in class, along with their students. Teachers who write with their students and read entries out loud in class lend credibility to the assignments; it is worth the teacher's time too. Doing the writing also tests the validity of the writing task; if the instructor has a hard time with a given topic, it provides an insight into the difficulties students may encounter and so makes for a better assignment next time.

The journal provides an easy means to evaluate each class session; the journal is not the only way to do this, of course, but it proves a handy place to keep these records, alongside the planning sessions and the inclass journal-writes. One of my own entries, for example, written ten minutes after class read like this:

> 12/16—9:40 a.m.—Union
>
> Class discussion of Orwell: asked small groups of people pointed questions and passages to look at for 15 minutes—then had people repeat to larger group. This started slow—but by last several reports, people were regularly contributing to the discussion. "Absence" continued to be a problem, with certain people missing frequently—screws up the groups and the presentations—the guy from group 2 who took the transparency home with him—he never showed up with it!
>
> Last 15 minutes of class: we projected one overhead and a second group orally explained their project. This was rushed and unsatisfactory; resolve to "start" next class with group work and discussion.
>
> Next class: I need to do certain things:
>   1. Finish *1984* discussion
>   2. Group projects
>   3. Allow group planning time in class
>   4. Collect papers (due)
>   5. Assign *Mythologies*
>
> Thursday Class
>
> 8:00: Meet in groups and discuss project
>   prepare outline of planned activities for me

8:30: Project 3 group plans for investigation
9:00: *1984* discussion: centered on "communication" and "human
    nature"

Jottings like this may help teachers understand better their own teaching process and sometimes result in useful insights about what should or shouldn't have been done. These evaluations also act as prefaces for the next planning session, pointing toward more structure or less. And when a class, for one reason or another, has been a complete failure, writing about it can be therapeutic; I, at least, try to objectify what went wrong and so create the illusion, at least, of being able to control it the next time.

Reading and Evaluating Student Journals

Reading student journals keeps teachers in touch with student experiences—frustrations, anxieties, problems, joys, excitements. Teachers who are aware of the everyday realities—both mental and physical—of student life may be better teachers because they can tailor assignments and tests more precisely to student needs. In other words, reading student journals humanizes teachers.

Some teachers insist on not reading student journals, arguing they have no right to pry in these private documents. It is a good point. However, there are important reasons why the teacher ought to look at the journals, and there are precautions which can eliminate prying. First, for students just beginning to keep journals, a reading by a teacher can help them expand their journals and make them more useful. Sometimes first journals have too many short entries; a teacher who notices this can suggest trying full-page exercises to encourage a fuller development of ideas. Second, some students believe that if an academic production is not reviewed by teachers it has no worth; while there is more of a problem here than reading journals, the teachers may decide at the outset that looking at the journals will add needed credibility to the assignment. Third, students feel that journals must "count for something"—as must every requirement in a high school or college setting. "If teachers don't look at these things how can they count 'em?"

One way to count a journal as part of the student's grade is to count pages. Some teachers grade according to the quantity of writing a student does: one hundred pages equals an 'A'; seventy-five a 'B'; fifty a 'C'; and so on. Other teachers attempt to grade on the quality of insight or evidence of personal growth. Still other teachers prefer a credit/no credit arrangement: to complete the requirements for the course the students must show evidence they have kept a journal.

Teachers need only see that pages of journal writing exist; they don't need to read the entries. While fair, this method precludes the teacher from learning through the students' writing.

To resolve this apparent paradox between the students' need for a private place to write and the benefit to both student and teacher from a public reading, I ask students to keep their journals in a loose-leaf format and to provide cardboard "dividers" to separate sections of the journal. I am able thus to look at sections dealing with my course, but not to see more personal sections. And if portions of the student's commentary about a particular class would prove embarrassing, the loose-leaf allows deletion of that entry prior to my perusal. I may ask for the pages concerning "American Literature," for example, the third week of the term, skim quickly, and hand back—making suggestions only to those students who are not gaining much from the experience. At the end of the course I may check the journals again and assign a credit/no credit mark. Or I may raise student grades for good journals (lots of writing), but not penalize students for mediocre ones.

Teachers who read journals need to be careful about how they respond to them. A small, positive comment following the latest entry encourages the writer to continue: "Good journal. I especially enjoyed your entry on freedom of speech." Date the comments and read from that point next time. Needless to say, negative or critical comments have no place.

Near the end of the term I usually ask students to prepare their journals for a public reading, to delete any entries too personal to share, and then add page numbers and a table of contents for major entries.[12] Finally, students write an entry in which they formally evaluate their own journal: "Which entries make the greatest impact on you now? Which seem least worthwhile? What patterns do you find from entry to entry?" For some students this proves to be the clarifying activity of the term, the action which finally defines the journals. For many, this informal, nongraded writing is a new and pleasant experience. In the words of one student:

> The journal to me has been like a one-man debate, where I could write thoughts down and then later read them, this seemed to help clarify many of my ideas. To be honest there is probably fifty percent of the journal that is nothing but B.S. and ramblings to fulfill assignments, but, that still leaves fifty percent that I think is of importance. The journal is also a time capsule. I want to put it away and not look at it for ten or twenty years and let it recall for me this period of my life. In the journal are many other things besides the writings, such as drawings and pages from this year's calendar. It is like a picture of this period of my life. When I continue writing a journal it will be of another portion of my life.

Conclusion

Journals are interdisciplinary and developmental by nature; it would be hard for writers who use journals regularly and seriously not to witness growth. I believe that journals belong at the heart of any writing-across-the-curriculum program. Journals promote introspection on the one hand and vigorous speculation on the other; as such they are as valuable to teachers in the hard sciences as to those in the more cushioned humanities. To be effective, however, journal use in one class ought to be reinforced by similar use in another class. Of course, for teachers in some disciplines, where the primary focus is the student's grasp of specialized knowledge, the personal nature of journals may be of secondary importance. However, the value of coupling personal with academic learning should not be overlooked; self-knowledge provides the motivation for whatever other knowledge an individual seeks. Without an understanding of who we are, we are not likely to understand fully why we study biology rather than forestry, literature rather than philosophy. In the end, all knowledge is related; the journal helps clarify the relationship.

Notes

1. Don Fader argues in favor of a program called "English in Every Classroom" in *Hooked on Books* (New York: Medallion, 1966); the student journal was a key component in his program. See also, James Britton, Tony Burgess, Nancy Martin, Alex McLeod, and Harold Rosen, *The Development of Writing Abilities (11–18)* (London: Macmillian Education, 1975); and Janet Emig, "Writing as a Mode of Learning," *College Composition and Communication* 28 (May 1977): 122–127.

2. Ken Macrorie, *Writing to Be Read*, 2nd ed. (Rochelle Park, N.J.: Hayden, 1976), p. 151.

3. Peter Elbow, *Writing without Teachers* (New York: Oxford University Press, 1973), p. 9.

4. Macrorie, p. 158.

5. Mark Hanson, *Sources* (Lakeside, Calif.: INTERACT, 1978).

6. Examples of journal use are taken from professors at Michigan Tech who have attended writing-across-the-curriculum workshops. For further information, contact the author.

7. Margaret Watson, *Mathematics Teacher* (October 1980), pp. 518–519.

8. Robert Stinson, "Journals in the Geography Class," *WLA Newsletter*, no. 15 (Findlay College, Spring, 1980): 5.

9. Teachers and counselors will find a thorough discussion of the possible therapeutic uses of personal journals in Ira Progoff's *At a Journal Workshop: The Basic Text and Guide for Using the Intensive Journal* (New York: Dialogue House, 1975).

10. Robert A. Rennert, "Values Clarification, Journals, and the Freshman Writing Course," *On Righting Writing*, ed. Ouida H. Clapp (Urbana, Ill.: NCTE, 1975), p. 196.

11. Robert Hawley, Sidney Simon, and D. D. Britton, *Composition for Personal Growth* (New York: Hart, 1973), p. 142.

12. I learned to organize journals from Dixie Goswami at the NEH Seminar "Writing in the Learning of Humanities," Rutgers University, New Brunswick, New Jersey, July 1977.

3 Writing and Problem Solving

Carol Berkenkotter
Michigan Technological University

Problem solving is common ground for all the disciplines and fundamental to all human activities. A writer is a problem solver of a particular kind. Writers "solutions" will be determined by how they frame their problems, the goals they set for themselves, and the means or plans they adopt for achieving those goals.

The relationship between writing and problem solving has been most recently examined in the research of Linda S. Flower and John R. Hayes.[1] Flower and Hayes are among a number of researchers in diverse fields who have studied the cognitive processes of experts and novices thinking aloud on tape as they solved problems in mathematics, physics, chess playing, and composing.[2] The findings in all of these areas point to a common conclusion: whether the problem solver is a writer, a musician, a physicist, or a chess player, experts appear to have an arsenal of strategies which will direct them toward a seminal (if not final) solution. Novices, on the other hand, most often rely on trial and error. A novice chess player, for example, might randomly try a variety of moves in a chess problem; an expert, in contrast, will employ a powerful strategy, such as "try to control the center of the board," drawing from long term memory a pattern which matches the configuration on the board. Similarly, novice writers when given a composing task will simply begin writing while thinking aloud, hoping for the "right" sentence that will carry them through the whole written draft. Expert writers, like expert chess players, are able to draw strategies from long term memory which put them in "control of the board." These strategies involve setting and resetting goals, generating ideas, exploring their relationships, and finally connecting them in some kind of analytic framework aimed at a specific reader.

Although differing in theoretical assumptions and research methodology,[3] Flower and Hayes share with James Britton the view that writing involves highly complex cognitive processes. In heeding the research findings of those attempting to track these processes, we are

33

beginning to devise pedagogical techniques that help students tap their own tacit resources. This essay presents suggestions on how current research on problem solving can be put to use in writing as well as other content area courses. The first section demonstrates how a problem-solving approach can be used in a composition course; the ensuing section offers practical suggestions for using writing as a problem-solving tool in other disciplines.

A Problem-Solving Approach to Writing

Can strategies that experts use be taught to beginning writers? The question is not an easy one to answer because an expert will have both experience and procedural knowledge to draw upon as well as composing strategies. However, the research of Flower, Hayes, and Nancy Sommers (who has studied the revision strategies of expert and novice writers)[4] suggests that the techniques that experienced writers use can be modified for the classroom.

In fact a number of strategies have been adapted for both beginning and advanced writers based on the following assumptions: (1) Effective writing is a goal-directed, hierarchically organized, recursive process which requires an awareness of the relationship between subject, purpose, and audience. (2) A writer has literally dozens of constraints to juggle simultaneously, among them lexical and syntactic decisions, tone, diction, organization, not to mention the larger rhetorical problems. (3) Trying to write under the pressure of too many constraints frequently creates "writer's block." It is necessary to break the composing process down into a number of subprocesses which include setting goals, making plans, generating ideas, and organizing the ideas into some kind of structure easily accessible to a particular audience. (4) There are strategies that will help guide the writer through each of these subprocesses.

Goal Setting and Planning

Goal setting is one useful strategy for getting students started with what they often view as a dreaded task. The general goal has already been set by the teacher: "Write about x (subject) for y (audience)." A number of questions will help a student determine further goals:

> What do you hope to accomplish with what you write?
>
> Satisfy the teacher?
>
> Convince y that x is true?
>
> Impress y by showing how much you know about x?
>
> Something else?

Setting goals will encourage students to develop plans, that is, to think about the method or means by which they will reach their goal. Typically, as students begin to write, their goals change and break down into smaller units or subgoals. As their goal base changes, they will restructure and adapt plans to fit their deepening understanding of the task at hand.

Setting goals and refining plans to meet them should not be confused with outlining, which impedes these processes. Outlines are inflexible; goal setting and planning should be fluid and flexible, suited to the students' changing awareness of what they want to say and why.

Strategies for Idea Generating

The act of writing begets ideas which help refine goals and reshape plans. Generating ideas—getting one's thoughts into words—requires the loosening up of information a writer has tucked away in long-term memory. One strategy for the retrieval of ideas is making lists by simply jotting down ideas as they come without worrying about tying them together into neat little bundles of sentences and paragraphs. Another technique for mental retrieval is "brainstorming," that is, breaking the class into groups so that everyone can contribute as many ideas as they can. Usually, one person's thoughts will act as a catalyst and "spark" others in the group. The following exercise combines both these techniques:[5]

1. Imagine that you are a consultant for a brickyard which makes common red construction bricks and is in financial difficulties. The manager of the brickyard is interested in new uses for his products and has asked you to provide him with some. Spend ten minutes or so thinking about the problem and then write down on a sheet of paper as many *new* uses for bricks as you can think of.

    (Were you aware of what went on in your mind when you were thinking about the problem? You probably did some type of ad-hoc listing of alteratives. However, your conceptualization may have suffered from lack of focus or from a premature judgment that rejected ideas which seemed impractical, or from labeling, choosing only commonplace ideas.)

2. Now take a blank piece of paper and spend four minutes listing all the uses you can think of for bricks. Try to avoid premature judgment and labeling.

3. Make a list of the attributes of a brick (weight, color, porosity, etc.). In groups, based on your lists of attributes, make a common

list of new uses for bricks. The rest of the class will then decide whether you are to receive a promotion or be fired.

Attribute listing is a strategy for developing greater fluency while getting ideas down. The brick exercise encourages students to think not only of what bricks as entities could be used for, but asks them additionally to break down their mental image of bricks. The listing of attributes should promote more (and wilder) ideas. In short, attribute listing helps overcome conceptual blocks that prevent the fullest expansion and flow of thoughts.

Another technique for releasing the flow of ideas is free writing. Free writing helps a writer turn off his or her mental "editor" (who is often preoccupied with the "good manners" of writing, such as spelling and grammar) and, as one writer who was trying to overcome a writing block put it, "free write your way to freedom." Furthermore, free writing allows one to hold considerations of form at bay and concentrate on getting down as many thoughts as possible. Two variations of free writing are, keeping a journal and "timed" or "shotgun" writings, which call for students to write down *everything* that is on their mind. During a "shotgun" exercise, the students are not to lift their pens from the paper; if they run out of things to say, they simply write "I have run out of things to say," until something pops into their head. Like listmaking, attribute listing, brainstorming, and journal writing, free writing helps students increase the output of ideas. After a sufficient quantity of ideas has been generated, they can go on to assess quality.

Developing Audience Awareness

Audience awareness, like goal setting, planning, and idea generating is recursive; that is, it is a matter of concern throughout the composing process. However, audience-directed strategies may be taught independently to help a class become aware of the fact that in "real world" writing there is a reader (other than the teacher) who should be taken very seriously. A clear sense of audience is just as important to the writing task as developing goals and plans, translating ideas into words, and organizing the material into some kind of logical structure.

A class should begin thinking about the identity of their reader even as an assignment is made. Questions similar to ones that Fred R. Pfister and Joanne F. Petrick asked their students will help fill out an image of the reader:

> What is his or her physical, social, and economic status? (age, environment, health, ethnic ties, class, income)
> What is his or her economic background?

What are his or her ethical concerns and values? (home, family, job success, religion, money, car, social acceptance)
What are his or her beliefs and prejudices?[6]

Once students have a concrete picture of their reader in mind, they should next consider how they want to affect the reader's thinking about their subject, and, finally, by what means they can best achieve their purpose. For example: If they are trying to get their audience to change an opinion, what tone do they want to use? What diction? How much information do they need to present? How can they best organize that information? How long and complex should their sentences be? All of these choices will grow from an analysis of the audience that progresses from questions that give the reader a real world identity to questions of *how* a writer can best present a subject to this reader.

A teacher I know uses the following deceptively simple exercise in a technical writing course to get his students to think precisely about the relationship between audience, subject, and purpose:

> You are to write the instructions for making a house from Lincoln Logs for the ten-to-twelve-year-old readers of *Jack and Jill* magazine.

He then brings the Lincoln Logs to class and role-plays a child following each set of instructions to the letter. The log house exercise vividly demonstrates to students the importance of a clear sense of audience.

Visualizing the Idea Structure

Listing, brainstorming, and free writing are powerful strategies for getting ideas on paper, but students will need another kind of strategy to help them organize their thoughts so that a reader can grasp the relationships among their ideas. A tree diagram or flow chart of ideas drawn after the students have done a free write or journal write or first draft will give them a visual representation of how their ideas may best be arranged into a tight structure. Figure 1 shows an "idea tree" by which an engineering student diagrammed his ideas for the assignment, "What makes writing difficult?" In a first draft this student had brainstormed effectively—so effectively that his paper was a morass of unrelated ideas on the sources of writing difficulties: "fear of writing," "lack of motivation," "no plan of attack," "poor vocabulary," "purpose of paper not defined." Class discussion brought out the fact that he knew his paper lacked organization, yet he had no means for pulling his ideas together. I asked him to use the tree structure to visually rank the ideas in the paper, beginning with the most inclusive.

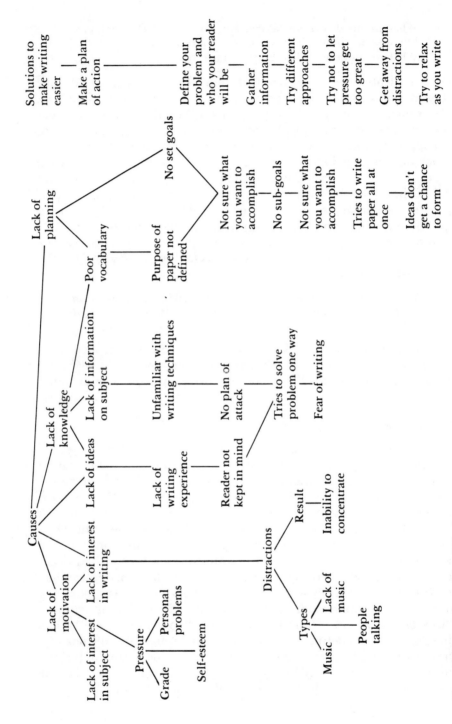

Figure 1. What makes writing difficult.

Writers can learn to use this strategy by analyzing someone else's writing first; for example, by diagramming the underlying idea structure in a long editorial in a newspaper or in an essay in a rhetoric reader. After students begin to feel comfortable with the technique ask them to use it on their own work. Chances are, they won't find as well developed an idea structure. If the ideas do not connect to each other or if the tree looks pretty bare, this means they need to do some rearranging and perhaps some more goal setting and idea generating.

Representing ideas graphically in an idea tree creates a hierarchical structure, that is, a structure which shows the relationship between superordinate and subordinate ideas. Students with some background in computer science find the flow chart a handy way to visualize idea relationships—though the flow chart, unlike the idea tree, is a closed system. The point is—whatever the technique—visualization facilitates the organization of ideas, which, in turn, helps to make them more easily accessible to a reader.

In summary, asking questions to set goals, making lists of ideas and attributes, brainstorming, free writing to get ideas flowing, developing a clear picture of the reader through the use of questions, and graphically representing the underlying idea structure of prose are all strategies to aid writers as they compose. These strategies are not rule-governed procedures that guarantee a solution. They do offer a high probability of success, or as Flower and Hayes point out, "formulize the efficient procedures a good journalist or scientist would use unconsciously."[7] The problem-solving approach to teaching writing gives a student a set of techniques useful in any course.

Writing and Problem Solving in Other Disciplines

The discovery function of writing in the content areas, particularly in the scientific and technological fields, can help students become aware of the processes they use to solve problems. Writing does this because, as James Britton has shown, "an essential part of the writing process is explaining the matter to oneself."[8] A colleague of mine, an engineer, asked his students to keep a journal, first to reflect on their preparatory reading before class, and then to summarize key concepts following the lecture. To his surprise, students produced flow charts, diagrams, and drawings integrated with their written responses. The students' journals illustrate a critical point: Because the professor was himself engaged in solving problems using what James L. Adams calls "alternate thinking languages"[9] (drawings, equations, slides), it was only natural that the students would respond in kind. The journal provided them with a medium for switching back and forth between verbal and visual modes of thought.

However, students are not often encouraged to write for discovery purposes outside of their composition courses; nor are they taught to develop fluent and flexible thinking habits through the use of alternate languages as they work through problems. Consequently, faculty are confronted by students who claim they "hate writing" and who depend on the textbook to arrive at solutions to math, science, and engineering problems. One response to this curricular dilemma is to make the use of visual techniques such as tree diagrams and flow charts part of writing instruction across the curriculum. This will give students experience verbalizing the subject matter they are ordinarily taught to think about only in equations, formulas, or other nonverbal modes. The following writing strategies are intended for use in disciplines in which writing is usually not associated with course content.

Keeping a Strategy Notebook

Most problem solvers switch from one strategy to another in working toward a solution, sometimes without conscious awareness of what they are doing. A strategy notebook offers students an array of problem solving techniques from which to choose. James L. Adams, a teacher of design in the Engineering School of Stanford University, explains why this is desirable: "First by selecting strategies consciously one can often find approaches he would never have known about had he left the selection to his subconscious. Secondly, by becoming aware of various thinking strategies, what they can do, and how to use them, one can ensure that the mind has a larger selection when it utilizes its subconscious selection method."[10]

A strategy notebook might include a brief listing of conventional problem-solving methods such as induction, deduction, reduction/combination (breaking a problem down into subproblems) and analogy. *Strategy Notebook*, published by Interaction Associates, lists some sixty-six strategies accompanied by a description of each.[11] These strategies include:

Build up	Relax	Search	Transform
Eliminate	Dream	Select	Translate
Work Forward	Imagine	Plan	Expand
Work Backward	Purge	Predict	Reduce
Associate	Incubate	Assume	Exaggerate
Classify	Display	Question	Understate
Generalize	Organize	Hypothesize	Adapt
Exemplify	List	Guess	Substitute
Compare	Check	Define	Combine

Relate	Diagram	Symbolize	Separate
Commit	Chart	Stimulate	Change
Defer	Verbalize	Test	Vary
Leap In	Visualize	Play	Cycle
Hold Back	Memorize	Manipulate	Repeat
Focus	Recall	Copy	Systemize
Release	Record	Interpret	Randomize
Force	Retrieve		

Using the notebook as a source, an instructor might ask students to keep track of the strategies they are using at any time during a problem-solving activity. Students might also keep a strategy notebook inductively—to list strategies as they arise while the student goes through the step by step procedure of solving a problem. The notebook would, in either case, serve as a resource for strategies to use when a student is in trouble or seeking alternative approaches.

Focus on Conceptualization

Arthur Whimbey and Jack Lochhead have developed a technique that fosters verbal conceptualization by asking physics and math students to work in pairs on verbal reasoning problems. As one student works a problem, the other asks a series of questions aimed at getting the problem solver to verbalize the mental processes he or she is going through—a step at a time. The questioners are told to keep the problem solvers talking as they work in order to make them aware of what they are thinking at all times. Then the pair trades roles as they work another problem.

The following problem and solution is typical of the material Whimbey and Lochhead use with their students.

Problem

On a certain day I ate lunch at Tommy's, took out two books from the library (*The Sea Wolf* and *Martin Eden*, both by Jack London), visited the museum, and had a cavity filled. Tommy's is closed on Wednesday, the library is closed on weekends, the museum is only open Monday, Wednesday and Friday, and my dentist has office hours Tuesday, Friday and Saturday. On which day of the week did I do all these things?

Solving the Problem

Step 1. Suggestion for beginning the problem: The restrictions on when these activities occurred are stated in the second sentence.

Step 2. Tommy's is closed on Wednesday . . .

       S   M   T ~~W~~ TH F SAT

Step 3. . . . the library is closed on weekends . . .

      ~~S~~ M T ~~W~~ TH F ~~SAT~~

Step 4. . . . the museum is only open Monday, Wednesday and
   Friday . . . This means it is closed the other days.
              ~~S~~ M ~~T~~ ~~W~~ ~~TH~~ F ~~SAT~~
Step 5. . . . and my dentist has office hours Tuesday, Friday and
   Saturday. This eliminates Monday.
              ~~S~~ ~~M~~ ~~T~~ ~~W~~ ~~TH~~ F ~~SAT~~
Step 6. On which day of the week did I do all these things: Friday.[12]

Using Polya's Check List

In addition to asking students to use writing/talking to keep track of
how they solve problems, a notebook can be used to record responses
to a check list of problem-solving procedures, such as those developed
by the mathematician George Polya in *How to Solve It.* Polya frames
a series of questions directed toward four goals: (1) understanding the
problem, (2) finding the connection between the data and the unknown
(which may involve considering auxiliary problems if an immediate
connection cannot be found) in order to eventually obtain a *plan* of
the solution, (3) carrying out the plan, (4) examining the solution
obtained (checking back). The questions include:

> Understanding the Problem
> *What is the unknown? What are the data? What is the condition?*
> Is it possible to satisfy the condition? Is the condition sufficient
> to determine the unknown? Or is it insufficient? Or redundant? Or
> contradictory?
> Separate the various parts of the condition. Can you write them
> down?
>
> Devising a Plan
> Have you seen the same problem in a slightly different form?
> *Do you know a related problem?*
> Look at the unknown! And try to think of a familiar problem
> having the same or a similar unknown.
> Could you restate the problem? Could you restate it still differently?
> Go back to definitions.
> If you cannot solve the proposed problem try to solve first some
> related problem. Could you imagine a more accessible related
> problem? A more general problem? A more special problem? An
> analogous problem? Could you solve a part of the problem?
> Did you use all the data? Did you use the whole condition?
> Have you taken into account all essential notions involved in the
> problem?
>
> Carrying Out the Plan
> Carrying out your plan of the solution *check each step.* Can you
> see clearly that the step is correct?
>
> Looking Back
> Can you check the result? Can you check the argument?
> Can you see [the result] at a glance?
> Can you use the result, or the method, for some other problem?[13]

Polya's questions themselves suggest strategies. They direct a student to break a problem down by setting a series of goals and subgoals, to use analogy, to develop plans, and to consider alternative solution procedures. Moreover, the questions invite responses that evoke verbal, visual, and mathematical notation. Like the strategy notebook and the Whimbey/Lochhead questioning technique, the check list is a discovery tool—it helps students to conceptualize their mental processes while they are actively engaged in solving problems.

The techniques of using writing interactively with visual and mathematical notation in a journal or notebook and of asking students to think aloud while solving problems have several heuristic functions: developing fluency and flexibility as students become adept at using alternate thinking languages; fostering and facilitating creative thinking; making students conscious of the step-by-step processes they use as they solve problems; developing the ability to conceptualize in a variety of content areas.

These last two functions may be particularly important if students are to transfer general problem-solving strategies from one discipline to another. (As of this writing there are no studies of heuristic transfer; it is an area worthy of investigation.)

Good writers (and other problem solvers) have a large repertory of strategies to draw on. As a teacher my concern is with the practical application of these strategies in the classroom. The material in this chapter has several implications for teachers in *all* disciplines. To summarize:

> Writing as a problem-solving activity aims to make students self-conscious about the way they conceptualize.
>
> Self-consciousness about the way one solves problems (in writing or in other disciplines) leads to more effective conceptualization and, finally, becomes a strategy for solving problems.
>
> Good problem-solving strategies cross disciplinary lines; in writing they become a means for producing effective prose; in other content areas writing can become one among many strategies for learning.

Notes

1. See "Problem-Solving Strategies and the Writing Process," *College English* 39 (December 1977): 451; "The Cognition of Discovery: Defining a Rhetorical Problem," *College Composition and Communication* 31 (February 1980): 21–32. From their research Flower and Hayes have developed a theory and model of writing as a cognitive process. See *A Process Model of Composition,* Technical Report No. 1, Document Design Project funded by the National

Institute for Education (Carnegie-Mellon University, 1979): 400-78-0043; "A Cognitive Process Theory of Writing," a paper presented at the Conference on College Composition and Communication, Washington, D.C., March 1980.

2. This method of research, protocol analysis, is a sequential record of a subject's behavior while actively engaged in performing a task. Typically, a protocol includes a transcript of a tape recording made by the subject who has been asked to verbalize his or her thinking process as well all notes, drawings, and written material.

3. Flower and Hayes differ from Britton in the nature of their writing models: Britton's linear model represents a series of stages separated in time: conception/incubation/production. [See James Britton, Tony Burgess, Nancy Martin, Alex McLeod, and Harold Rosen, *The Development of Writing Abilities (11-18)* (London: Macmillan Education, 1975).] In contrast, the Flower/Hayes model is recursive—at any time in the writing process, any or all elements of that process may be brought into play. For example, when writers are reviewing they may find that they are setting new goals and plans. In this sense the process is cyclical rather than linear.

4. See "Revision Strategies of Student Writers and Experienced Adult Writers," *College Composition and Communication* 31 (May 1980): 378–388.

5. James L. Adams has developed this modification of J. P. Guilford's "brick use" test in *Conceptual Blockbusting* (New York: W. W. Norton, 1978), p. 79, a book that identifies various conceptual blocks and proposes strategies for overcoming them.

6. "A Heuristic Model for Creating a Writer's Audience," *College Composition and Communication* 31 (May 1980): 214.

7. "Problem-Solving Strategies and the Writing Process," *College English* 39 (December 1977): 451.

8. Britton, p. 28.

9. Adams, pp. 93-111.

10. Adams, p. 68.

11. Adams, p. 66.

12. *Problem-Solving and Comprehension: A Short Course in Analytic Reasoning* (Philadelphia: The Franklin Institute Press, 1979), pp. 57-60.

13. Adams, pp. 89-90; adapted from George Polya, *How to Solve It: A New Aspect of Mathematical Method* (Princeton, N.J.: Princeton University Press, 1945), pp. 6-15.

4 Assigning and Evaluating Transactional Writing

Toby Fulwiler
Michigan Technological University

Robert Jones
Michigan Technological University

Transactional writing is writing to get things done, to inform or persuade a particular audience to understand or do something. This most common category of school writing is also most commonly demanded in the world of work—in corporations, industries, and bureaucracies. In school such writing is exemplified by book reviews, term papers, laboratory reports, research projects, masters proposals, and doctoral dissertations; outside school, such writing takes the form of letters, memos, abstracts, summaries, proposals, reports, and planning documents of all kinds. Students who practice transactional forms of writing in their classroom will have lots of opportunities to practice it on their jobs. It is important, therefore, that students learn to do it well—clearly, correctly, concisely, coherently, and carefully.

We believe that all classroom teachers are, to some extent, language teachers. They all play a role in how students view writing; they play this role subtly when they make writing assignments and more obviously when they evaluate those assignments. How teachers assign and respond to transactional writing has a lot to do with whether or not students value it and how well they learn to produce it. Consider, for example, the following situations:

> A paper is written as extra credit in a geography class; it is due at the end of the semester and has as its subject "The Forests of North America." The paper is mechanically competent (spelling and punctuation are fine), but the five pages of writing are unfocused, generalized, and superficial.

> A take-home examination in history is handed in after being assigned the previous day. The paper has numerous spelling mistakes, misused commas, and a few fragment sentences. The answers, while not wrong, are general and wordy.

45

> A technical report is turned in by a sophomore enrolled in a chemistry class; it is her first such report, and much of the information is presented incorrectly: the conclusion is at the end; the "discussion" is written in first person; no "abstract," "table of contents," nor "sub-headings" is provided.

For instructors under time and workload constraints, the easiest response to each "poor paper" is a low grade. However, while 'D' and 'F' are easy and common responses, they are not necessarily effective in changing behavior, nor really efficient—if succeeding papers show no improvement.

Grading poor writing has about the same effect as grading poor test answers; it measures the specific performance, but does not result in improved learning. Since writing is a skill which takes a long time to master fully, simply assigning low grades cannot be very effective writing pedagogy. Instructors who want to be more helpful in their responses to poor writing might begin by asking themselves questions about each writing assignment. The preceding three examples suggest some possible lines of inquiry.

The geography instructor might ask: (a) Did I ask the student to explore his topic with me in advance? (b) Did I (or anyone else) see or critique a first draft? (c) Did I ask for a first draft? (d) Have I explored the nature of library research with my class or this student? (e) What options have I left for the student, now that the semester is over?

The history professor might ask: (a) How long did the student spend writing this paper? (b) Are the mistakes due to ignorance or carelessness? (c) How many spelling mistakes, such as "thier" and "hisory," are really typos? (d) Is my best response an "F," a conference, or a request for revision? (e) Do I want to "test" the student's knowledge, "teach" academic discipline, or "motivate" the student to learn more history?

The chemistry teacher might ask: (a) Does this student know how science reports differ from history term papers? (b) Did I explain the requirements for this report orally or in writing? (c) Do my students know the logic behind scientific reporting? (d) Is the first person always forbidden in report writing? (e) Is my best response a low grade, a conference with the individual, or a conversation with the whole class?

Serious instructors *do* ask questions about the causes of poor student writing. They do not often find simple answers, though, because writing and the teaching of writing involve complicated processes. Teachers interested in better student writing must begin with questions such as these: What do I want my students to learn? How can I prepare my students to write better? How should I evaluate a piece of writing?

The following sections are intended to show how these questions might be answered.

Writing and Learning

We are all familiar with student writing problems, problems due to poor composing skills, insufficient knowledge, immature thinking, and lack of interest—to name a few. But what about the problems caused by teachers? Is it possible that some of the problems are teacher-centered rather than student-centered? We're thinking here about vague or poorly explained directions on a writing assignment; exam questions which make false assumptions about what students know or should know; assignments which do not challenge students and are perceived as dull, repetitious, or tedious; incomplete or harmful responses by teachers to student writing; and poor planning, timing, or sequencing of assignments. These are but some of the ways that teachers, without malice and with good intentions, may affect the quality of student writing by poor assignments and ill-considered response to that writing.

Teachers often spend days in preparation and even weeks (or units) talking about, demonstrating, and explaining information to students; the same teachers, however, may not spend much time thinking about how writing can assist in both the learning and evaluating of that information. For example, one social studies teacher told me that she made "essay question" assignments when she didn't have time to compose a good objective test. This is not necessarily a poor or lazy decision on the teacher's part—depending, of course, on class context, among other things. In fact, the decision to ask for a long student answer from a brief teacher question seems to be a simple time trade-off when compared to a short student answer in response to a long teacher question. The objective test, so long in the making, is short in correcting; the essay test, short in the making, will be longer in correcting. But, of course, this decision involves something more complex than merely juggling time.

Asking for the student's answer *in writing* should be an important pedagogical decision, not simply a trade-off in time. In the objective test the teacher does most of the careful conceptual work, thinking through how best to create choices and how to word those choices. In the essay test, the situation is reversed, with the student being asked both to make choices and to choose the words. To *compose* something is a more demanding task—coordinating knowledge with both logic and rhetoric—for the student than simply *deciding* (or guessing at) something. Asking for a piece of writing involves students more profoundly in the learning process; they must demonstrate not only "knowledge" but also the ability to organize and explain that knowledge.

The teacher who asks "What do I want students to learn" will assign writing that is most likely to generate a specific form of learning. For example, different question types call for different kinds of responses. If we ask the "date" on which the Vietnam War started, the answer ought to be a matter of simple *recall*—something learned somewhere and now recalled. If we ask for a list of the chief "causes" of the war, recall is involved but also some choices and some *analysis* ("This cause is more important than that cause"). Third, if we ask about the relationship between the war and the women's movement, a great deal of information must be *synthesized* to arrive at a coherent, believable answer. Finally, if we ask whether it was right or wrong that America became involved in Vietnam, a *judgment* based on some standard or other is called for.

These four different test objectives—recall, analysis, synthesis, judgment—suggest in concrete terms the manner in which the teacher's question determines the kind of thinking students must do. If it is important that social studies students learn to analyze, then teacher questions ought to reflect that; if humanities students must learn to express and defend value judgments, their teachers may aid that process by asking judgmental questions. Only in the area of simple recall would the essay seem to have little advantage over the short answer.

Preparing Assignments

Most teachers realize through personal experience that most acts of writing represent stages in a larger process: that is, whether the writing is an answer to an essay question, a preliminary draft of a formal paper, or a response to a class question, it represents only one point along a continuum. The poet William Wordsworth said that poetry is the "spontaneous overflow of emotion recollected in tranquility," but he still revised some of his poems dozens of times. Though we cannot ask for twelve revisions of a piece of student writing, we can learn an important principle from Wordsworth's practice: Any act of writing involves a multistage process of thinking, rethinking, writing, rewriting, and editing. We can and should provide an academic environment where students see this clearly.

General principles for making good assignments evolve directly from understanding the *process* of composition—what happens when human beings put words on paper. While each specific assignment depends on course content, teacher personality, student skills, and everybody's time and energy, teachers who keep the writing process in mind will help their students learn to write better.

When we stop to think about it, we quickly realize that the act of writing is complicated, certainly more involved than simply putting down on paper what's already in the writer's head. We seldom begin writing with well-formed sentences and paragraphs in our heads already. To understand the word "process" as applied to writing, it is only necessary to think through all the thoughts and activities associated with our own formal writing activities: we need to have (1) a purpose for writing in mind and (2) an audience to write to. We further need to (3) find an idea, (4) refine and incubate that idea, (5) write it down in words, (6) organize and reshape it, (7) try it out on a trial audience and receive feedback, which often necessitates (8) rewriting or revising that idea, (9) editing, and finally (10) proofreading—then sometimes starting all over again because new information now modifies our prior assumptions. Of course, the writing process is not "Ten Steps" as this list implies, nor is it sequential and orderly, but these hypothetical steps do indicate some of the factors common to school writing tasks.

Teachers aware of the composing process use this knowledge in making, intervening in, and evaluating writing assignments. Consider the following suggestions:

1. Find out in advance how much students know and don't know about the kind of writing you are asking for. Do they know what a research paper is and how it differs from a book report or personal opinion paper? Discuss these differences.

2. Lead up to assignments with deliberate invention techniques, including oral brainstorming, free writing, and journal writing. Most of us who have graduated from college have learned, often the hard way, to write notes to ourselves, outline, and talk with others to get our writing started in the right direction; we can teach our students to use these techniques to start their writing assignments.

3. Try to stimulate personal involvement between writer and writing assignments. This can be done not only by giving a variety of choices in topics but also by engaging students in dialogues about potential topics and asking them to keep journals—dialogues with themselves—about what is important to them and what not.

4. Create class contexts for writing assignments so that the topic grows from a prepared culture. For example, bring in outside speakers on the topic, take context-producing field trips, assign

and discuss relevant readings, and engage in a lot of clarifying class discussion.

5. Pose problems to the class—or ask the class to help pose problems. Use the blackboard or overhead projector liberally in this process so that problems in need of written solution are visually clear and precise. Ask students to consider papers as "solutions" to these problems. This approach exemplifies what a "thesis" is and how it may be supported or proven.

6. Assign several short papers during the term rather than one long one at the end. You can find out an enormous amount about the students' grasp of conventions and organizing abilities in a two-page paper (300–500 words); assigning it means you will have more time to respond to each paper and to make suggestions that can be followed up in the next assignment.

7. Ask for multiple drafts of papers, if you have the chance—even short two-page papers become more effective learning projects when students are asked to (or allowed to) revise them according to specific critical suggestions.

8. Explain what you expect from each writing assignment in advance and evaluate accordingly. If you are concerned that students do a particular kind of research on an assignment, how well they report and explain that research ought to be the primary trait determining the students' grades. In an assignment meant to be carried through several drafts, the teacher can sequence these expectations: first draft is most concerned with organizing and structuring an idea; second draft is more concerned with use of supporting examples, and so on. Students should always understand clearly what is expected of them.

9. Show students models of student-written papers. This will give them a concrete sense of how the assignment might be fulfilled. Some teachers create files of good samples from previous classes; others use published examples; a very few show their own writing about the assignment to students. Models give students confidence that the assignment *can* be done because it *has* been done and show them that there might be several solutions to the writing problem.

10. If you get bored by sameness and dullness when reading a pile of student papers, make it clear when making an assignment that students who take some risks to be original will be rewarded—or at least not penalized. Some students will not trust you the first time on this, but passing out samples of successful "risk" papers may encourage the cautious to try new things.

This discussion has been concerned primarily with formal writing assignments which students do outside of class. While the manner in which the teacher structures the assignment plays a significant role in how well the student handles the assignment, the students' responsibility is considerable; we expect their papers to display an organized knowledge of the topic in clear, concise, correct, and coherent prose. We must modify those expectations when we ask students to write in class.

Essay Tests

The essay examination is a common way to use writing in liberal arts classrooms. It provides teachers with a means of checking the student's knowledge and ideas while also determining whether the student can express them in a well organized manner. Though essay answers are usually first draft efforts, we often treat them otherwise. Professional writers do not expect correct error-free writing on first drafts. Neither should we. Essay examinations can be a sound educational tool, but, like more formal assignments the students must be prepared to take them.

Teachers can provide students with the opportunity to practice answering the questions and establish models and standards by which the writer's work will be evaluated. We would not expect the piano student to perform and be evaluated without practice and a chance to hear the piece played correctly. Yet many of us simply assume that our students know intuitively how to write clear answers to complex questions.

The following suggestions, based on work with teachers in various disciplines, are designed to help students understand better what is expected on essay examinations.

Sample question. Provide a few minutes of class time occasionally to write an answer to a sample essay question. If the essay examinations you give are based on class discussions, this practice can match the overall goals for any given course. For example, an ecology class may have been discussing the conflict of pollution and progress in a town which suffers from acute unemployment. Asking the student to take a few minutes to organize in writing the particulars of each position not only helps them clarify their perceptions of the conflict, but also helps them master the facts involved. Do they recall what studies have shown? Are they arguing from the facts rather than from the situation or *ad hominum*?

Peer groups. Ask students to share practice essay questions either in pairs or in small groups of three or four. Pairing and grouping of students encourages active learning. Too often lecture and textbook are our students' only access to information. When students can share ideas in small discussion groups, they are often more willing to inform, persuade, and challenge each other than they would be before an entire class.

Homework. Give a question as homework and then briefly go over the answers, making few comments. Without actually grading the paper, you can in a nonthreatening way simply acknowledge that a student has completed an assignment. You need not stress the same types of comments on each set of papers. Tell the students one time that you're looking closely at organization, another time that you are concerned with sentence construction. Over time the students will receive much needed practice in writing, which subtly enhances grammatical and mechanical competence as well as composition proficiency.

Model answers. Write an answer to a sample question before asking the students to answer it and share your effort with the class. Students are fond of this practice for several reasons. First, they see that you are willing to do the assignments that you require of them. Second, they get an idea of how a professional responds to this type of assignment; thus, they follow a model which demonstrates the fusing of both information and acceptable form. Third, they have a chance to critique the teacher's work, while the teacher has the advantage of seeing the assignment from the student's perspective. (Was the question clear? How hard was it for you to answer? Did you spend longer writing the answer than you expected?) In short, taking the role of the writer benefits both teacher and student.

Student samples. Show samples of student writing which exemplify strengths and weaknesses. Especially when viewed on an overhead or opaque projector, these papers provide a strong focus for comments from students and teacher. Moreover, you can clearly label strengths and note such problems as redundant words or ideas. Overhead projection of sample papers saves time because you don't have to create and pass out dittoed papers.

Expectations. Discuss with the students how different questions call for different kinds of reasoning; point out that "what" and "when" questions usually demand recall, while "how" and "why" questions usually demand more complicated types of thinking—analysis, synthesis, or judgment. Clarify to both your students and yourself what you want when you ask students to "discuss" or "explain"—each of these directions can be ambiguous.

The essay examination is a good means of testing students' knowledge, but without adequate preparation it can also be a source of frustration to both teacher and student. As the student becomes better prepared to write a soundly developed, clearly written answer, that frustration lessens. One last caution: No matter how much we prepare our students to write sound answers to essay questions, those answers will seldom match the quality of ones on which the students can spend more time revising and editing. The essay question asks for certain reasoning and writing skills; but it does not provide writers with a chance to demonstrate their comprehensive writing abilities as do more formal writing assignments.

Preparing students to write better by attending to the writing process both inclass and out goes a long way toward improving student writing. However, viewing writing as a "process" also modifies some traditional notions of evaluation. In the final section of this chapter we consider a variety of evaluative responses.

Evaluating Student Writing

Like "assignment making," the concept of "evaluation" makes a different kind of sense when placed in the context of writing as a process. Just as writing makes more sense when conceived with a variety of *audiences* in mind, from oneself through peers and the distant public, so too does evaluation make more sense when related to the various audiences that a piece of writing might have.

1. Students can learn certain response techniques to evaluate their own writing. (Teacher provided guide sheets, regularly required revision, etc.)

2. Students can learn to respond in nonthreatening, nonjudgmental ways to each other's writing. ("I was interested in this . . . I want more information on that.")

3. Teachers can explore nongraded responses to help students through different phases of the writing process. ("Can you elaborate on your argument on page two?")

4. Students can write for real public audiences and receive "evaluation" through an editor's acceptance or rejection. (Letters to the editor, essays in a school publication, professional newsletters, etc.)

Another way of looking at responses to writing, again suggested by a study of the whole composing process, is to consider what *function*, exactly, a piece of writing is meant to serve. Depending on what assignment a teacher makes, evaluation might take one form rather than another. For example, a teacher who asks for a research project due late in the term may incorporate evaluative responses at various steps along the way, as different aspects of research are undertaken by the students: library search techniques, information categorizing, documenting procedures, presentation of evidence, and so on. Each step in the process may suggest one critical intervention rather than another, including, for example, self-paced library worksheets, teacher review of research proposals, and peer critique of rough drafts. Or, by contrast, a teacher response to pieces of writing produced by an examination situation might require (traditionally) a single grade marked on the paper or (experimentally) a request for individual or collaborative revision and resubmission. In other words, a writing task suggests evaluative response.

The two major determiners that shape a piece of writing, audience and function, should determine the response to that piece of writing. Teachers who are aware of other parts of the composing process can also **discover** other appropriate points of intervention. At the conceptual stage, for example, large group brainstorming and small group critiques can help individual student writers get started. At the terminal stage of "proofreading," paired paper exchanges immediately prior to paper submission can help students eliminate annoying small errors. This helps (speeds) teacher reading and also teaches a valuable real-life writing technique, sharing a piece of writing with a colleague or spouse before sending it to a professional editor.

At the Michigan Tech writing workshops we commonly discuss principles of response and evaluation which teachers should keep in mind as they comment on and grade student papers. The following list of guidelines is the result of a discussion among a group of college teachers representing different disciplines across the campus:

1. Give positive feedback wherever possible. Even the most error-filled paper usually has something redeeming about it, a place where the writer, once encouraged, can get a new start. None of us feels like reworking a piece when *nothing* good is said about it.

2. Do not grade early drafts of a writing assignment. Putting a grade on a paper you want students to keep working on shuts down the incentive to revise; they read that shorthand evaluation ("D") rather than your written words. Grading something suggests finality and almost guarantees that the learning process, in this situation, has stopped.

3. Respond with specific suggestions for improvement wherever you can. "AWK" or "OUCH!" or "YUK" go only so far in telling the student what to do to make it better.

4. Create simple guidelines or self-critique sheets to help students respond more critically to their own writing—this may save you

time in the long run if they become adept at catching some of their own errors. Such sheets might ask, for example: What is your point? What is your pattern of organization? Have you supported all generalizations with specific examples? Do you avoid wordy construction, repetitive phrases, and clichés? Have you proofread for errors in spelling, punctuation, or typing?

5. Plan personal conferences for difficult or sensitive problems. In some cases, no amount of written commentary will bridge the gap between you and a misunderstanding student. The personal conference creates a human dimension to evaluation that writing cannot duplicate.

6. Give students some responsibility for evaluating each other's work; remember that each writer also benefits from becoming a critic and editor. (Guideline sheets similar to those in no. 4 work for pairs and small groups too.)

7. Don't separate form from content. Most writing is all of a piece; when a proposition is awkwardly stated it is often poorly understood. Consider the written expression as an integral part of the mental process; that way students will learn how the real world will, in fact, respond to them. (Consider also the appearance of a piece of writing as, to some extent, analogous to that which the writer personally presents to the world: sloppy and smudged or careful and clear?)

This chapter suggests that there is an important relationship between what we know about the composing process and (1) what we ask for on writing assignments, (2) how we prepare students to write our assignments, and (3) how we evaluate the writing that results. We feel confident that teachers who explore these relationships and translate them into solid pedagogical strategies will help their students write better formal papers and, at the same time, increase their students' abilities to reason and understand.

5 Audience and Purpose in Writing

Jack Jobst
Michigan Technological University

To most of us, the word "audience" presents an image of people in an auditorium applauding the efforts of an entertainer on stage. Certainly I would have used such a definition several years ago when I was a sophomore at Conestoga Senior High School in Berwyn, Pennsylvania. I took world history, then taught by the football coach, Mr. Antonio, a man of no great nuance. I had personal goals at that age, and since traditional methods of success seemed doubtful, I determined that I would gain worldly and social success as a comedian.

As I sat listening to my history class discuss the shipping trade in the Mediterranean Sea before Christ, I realized that my first opportunity was approaching. While I couldn't stand up in front of the group and perform, I could amaze them with a comic answer to one of the teacher's predictable questions. I guessed what question Mr. Antonio would ask and practiced my reply, polishing the subtleties of pause and inflection. I did not wait in vain, for on a clear October afternoon my opportunity arrived.

The Mediterranean test would be on Friday, and Antonio read through his list of review questions. Then it came.

"What are some contributions given us by the Phoenicians?" he asked. My hand waved like a sunflower among cabbages, and he nodded at me.

"Phoenician blinds," I said, carefully articulating and projecting my words so all in the classroom could hear. The roars of laughter washed over me from my appreciative audience, but I didn't allow this expected response to change my demeanor, for I knew that a good comic responded to his own gags with a deadpan.

The bell rang, and I heard Mr. Antonio say something about my being sharp as a marble, but I was not concerned with his attempt to diminish my limelight.

Out in the hallway, however, a classmate revealed that my careful planning had backfired when he asked why I thought the sailor-merchant Phoenicians had also worked on windows.

"That was a joke," I told him.
"Really?" he said. "When you didn't laugh I figured you were serious."

Although I had failed to understand my audience in that history classroom, I had made a distinguished effort. I neglected to realize that my reputation as a comic was not well established, and thus when I didn't laugh at my own remark, the other students interpreted my reply as serious. And stupid. I was correct, however, in believing that they would find humor in the juxtaposition of a modern window shade with an ancient culture. I am proud of my participation in that classroom of fifteen year olds because I had considered some complex elements of audience analysis, such as what humorous material the group would respond to and how a joke might best be communicated —in this case, as classroom dialogue between instructor and student.

Many students, I believe, also have an understanding of audience, but it is limited to oral rather than written communication. In my history class I was communicating in a familiar setting to people I knew. I was vividly aware of my classroom audience because they were present, and I had dealt with them numerous times before. If, on the other hand, I were writing a report on Phoenicians to local members of the National Geographic Society, I would feel much less secure because I had no experience with such an audience. Maxine Hairston makes the same point in *A Contemporary Rhetoric*: Students, she says, know enough to vary tone and argumentative methods when dealing with parents and peers, but given an audience that cannot be seen and does not provide immediate feedback, the communication produces material which is often meaningless to everyone but the writer.[1] In communicating orally, I as a student was aware of several audiences; but in written work, I could have named only one. The sole audience for my written work as a student was the adult in front of the room who ran the class and who regularly gave me essay tests. And generally found me wanting.[2]

From the research of James Britton we know that, depending upon the class level, students direct virtually all writing at an instructor who is viewed in one of two ways: as a "dialogue participant," or as an "examiner."[3] The stance which occurs earliest in a child's school experience is the "dialogue participant," in which the teacher is seen as friend, as someone interested in two-way learning through written communication. An example might be the encouraging notes an elementary teacher writes at the bottom of a work sheet, such as "I enjoyed the story you wrote about your brother," to which the student replies on the next submitted paper, "My brother didn't want me to tell that story, but I'm glad I did." This dialogue produces an attitude supportive of writing. Unfortunately, the opportunity and motivation for teacher/pupil dialogue diminishes, often because of teacher and curriculum policies, as the student rises through the class levels.

The second category may develop unnecessary fear and anxiety in student writers if the "teacher as examiner" is the sole focus of written communication. Britton points out that almost half of all student writing is from pupil to examiner, with all the pressures and anxieties inherent in such communication.[4] If writing, however, is used for activities in addition to grading, such as in journals, and in classes other than English, this anxiety may diminish.

Besides the problem with writing anxiety, students who write only for the "teacher as examiner" fail to learn methods of writing to other audiences. Clearly, this limited use of written communication ill prepares students for adult life, when they will be forced into dealing with numerous audiences. But it is difficult to bring audiences other than the teacher into a classroom, and students know that virtually all graded assignments are judged by the teacher, regardless of who is the "assigned" audience. Some instructors avoid this problem by sending the student-written material to outside graders in business and industry, but this solution is unavailable to most teachers.

Different audiences, however, may be simulated. A geography instructor might assign a report detailing the environmental conditions of southern Brazil and tell his students that they are to write for a hypothetical agricultural loan officer in the World Bank. The geography teacher begins his assignment by leading a class discussion identifying what a World Bank official expects in a report. Thus, while the students write for the instructor's approval, they nevertheless must compose their material for the target audience, and their work is judged on how well they meet those expectations.

Few beginning writers unfamiliar with audience analysis, however, could successfully complete the assignment of writing to a World Bank official without considerable help. A more practical approach to teaching audience is through a series of increasingly more complex assignments, beginning with relatively simple, easily-visualized readers, and moving toward audiences that are less familiar or more specialized. Such assignments would systematically lead students away from their inabilities to perceive audiences beyond themselves, a situation termed "cognitive egocentrism."[5] James Moffett speaks of this problem when he refers to an inexperienced writer's "assumption that the reader thinks and feels as he does, has had the same experience, and hears in his head when he is reading, the same voice the writer does when he is writing."[6]

The following assignments offer a variety of possibilities for teaching audience analysis. While few teachers may have the time to use all that is offered, a selection of two or three should provide students with an understanding of one of the most important considerations in communicating successfully. In a sense, studying audience might enlighten beginning writers much like sitting in a dark room, then raising the Phoenician blinds.

Audience in the Classroom

Before any communication is attempted, writers should first determine what information they possess. To assist them in generating ideas, instructors may assign journals and free writing, not only to bring forth possible writing ideas, but also to diminish the writers' anxiety about having something to say. I remember the fears which nearly always accompanied me during essay exams. No matter how much I had studied, I was still anxious when I first read the essay question. "Not this topic!" I thought to myself. "I didn't study this one enough." However, when I began writing, I discovered shelves of stored information waiting to be written down. Students often experience the same feeling—relief at discovering they have something to say. For the teacher, an added advantage of prewriting activities is the opportunity they present during class discussion to guide students away from trite material. Of course, the awareness of overused expressions and ideas is also part of audience analysis, for the knowledge of what is a cliché indicates that a writer knows what may potentially bore the reader/listener.

Prewriting need not be done on class time, but it should precede most assignments. The instructor might begin with a journal write asking the students to list some personality aspects of the target audience, such as age, personal interests, and educational background. For the more sophisticated assignments, the teacher could place the class in small groups, directing each to analyze one of the personality elements in more detail. Another group might contemplate suitable format for the discourse, and an appropriate tone.

One useful technique for introducing audience to the class is to distribute a questionnaire on the subject to determine class attitudes. The questions might first ask the students to explain their understanding of the term "audience" and then focus on the writer's need for such knowledge.[7]

1. List the different audiences for whom you have written in the past year, both in and out of school (for example, a particular relative, editor of the paper, school official, certain teacher, other).

2. Select two of the above audiences and briefly explain how you wrote differently for each.

3. How is a school newspaper article written differently from a book review for English class?

4. Why is the article written differently?

The results from such a questionnaire are not only useful in organizing class discussion, but they also automatically teach some of the principles behind audience analysis, such as shaping material for the reader. In other words, simply posing the problem of audience to a class will raise the level of audience awareness among class members.

The Interview

Interviews are important in many academic disciplines. Social and political scientists, for example, conduct polls to determine group attitudes and concerns, while journalists and researchers consider the interview an important tool for obtaining information. An exercise in interviewing also offers at least two advantages to the student of audience analysis: it diminishes writer's anxiety while simultaneously developing an understanding of audience.

To begin, the class might consider a journal entry describing what a newspaper reporter would ask a subject in order to write an interesting personality profile. In the discussion which follows, the teacher could guide the students away from overreliance on listing hobbies, place of birth, and the like towards revealing more vivid personality attributes, such as why the subject enjoys contact sports or cars. The interviewers should look for the unusual, that which sets the person apart from others.

Useful class discussion could also come from a study of professional interviews, such as those published in syndicated newspaper columns or national magazines, such as *Time* or *Newsweek*. Some teachers might select interviews from periodicals in their own disciplines, such as *Engineering Education,* then slant the assignment towards the special needs of their classes. Students could then discuss what segment of the article they found the most interesting and why. The people interviewed in periodicals are often controversial, and the class might benefit from a study of those questions dealing specifically with what is controversial: how are they worded, and in what order? Classmates are seldom controversial, of course, but nevertheless there is something which distinguishes everyone from the rest of humanity, and if the class is simulating a journalistic interview, the students' job is to discover that element and draw it out.

An alternative prewriting exercise consists of writing questions for distinguished personalities. The instructor writes on the board a list of names, say Darwin, Freud, Madame Curie, Shakespeare, and perhaps the local mayor or school president. The students should consider what questions they might ask one of those individuals, and explain *why* one question rather than another would be preferable.

In the discussion afterwards, the teacher could move the class towards an understanding of why they asked certain questions. The point is that they had a personal interest in certain topics, such as the school president's views on improving campus parking or raising tuition, or whether Madame Curie feels that the position of women in science has substantially improved since her lifetime.

Besides the opportunity of learning how to phrase questions, these two prewriting exercises produce an analysis of each individual student as audience, a looking inward at what each of them wants to and needs to know. They also provide understanding of what it is about certain topics that motivates a listener and a reader. The actual interview between students should take only about twenty minutes, with some additional time for the subjects to make comments about the interviewers' sketches, their factuality, appropriateness of tone, and so on. Finally, each reporter reads the article to the class or the other members of their smaller peer group. The follow-up discussion considers highlights of the better interviews, again searching for generalizations about why certain information is more interesting for the class to read.

This assignment is useful at the beginning of the school term because it allows classmates to become knowledgeable about each other. It also provides a writing situation which is nonthreatening; beginning writers fear being criticized, but less so from their peers, especially ones sitting across from them who have the same assignment to fulfill. Students often fear not having sufficient material to work with, but an interview generally produces a surfeit of information.

Writing Technical Directions

Practicing how to write directions is useful for students in scientific and technical subjects, for those areas require individuals with the ability to carefully describe experimental procedures. The following assignment has an extra advantage in that success or failure is immediately apparent when the students exchange their work and try to accomplish each other's directions. Here are some topics from which to choose:

Games

The instructor may divide the class into two groups or use two different classes. Each group will view the demonstration of a different simple game by an individual who will avoid "telling" how to play, although some elements, of course, must be verbalized, such as the object of play. No written information should be supplied that will shift the writers' reliance from themselves to the demonstrator. Student pairs might play once or twice before combining talents on writing the directions for their counterparts in the other group.

This assignment works best when uncomplicated games are selected, such as "penny pitching," and the old "bar" game involving thirteen match sticks. In the latter, either player may begin and select from one to three sticks, which are set aside. The opposing player then selects from one to three, and so on until the loser is left with the last stick.

Even if some students know these games, the assignment is still useful because the focus is not on the playing but on the articulation of how to play. The instructor should ask those reading the directions to act as if they have never played the game before, and to follow the directions exactly as written by the student authors.

Sandwich Making

Writing directions for making peanut butter and jelly sandwiches shares the advantages of the above ideas, but it doesn't involve multiple groups. The class completes directions for the sandwich, and the papers are then read aloud to a "chef" at the front of the room who, the class learns, is an alien with only a literal understanding of English. The chef follows the directions word-for-word, using the necessary sandwich components. Common mistakes include failing to consider the following: the kind of bread as white, rye, wheat, etc.; whether it is in whole loaf or slice form; how much of each ingredient is used; which utensils are required and when; and which comes first, the peanut butter, or the jelly.

Classroom Science Experiment

An alternative to the sandwich topic requires students to write directions explaining how to perform a simple experiment. The instructor discusses an experiment which is appropriate for the class level, and requests a set of directions containing sufficient detail so that someone not in the course could perform it. Afterwards, the instructor could perform the experiment from sample, student-written directions, identifying what common but necessary elements are often neglected in writing lab reports.

Follow Up

These writing assignments teach students that directions must not only consider the audience's skill level, but also any possible misinterpretations and pitfalls. The assignments are particularly useful when peer groups are used to aid in understanding and promote learning.

Some students will employ visuals and other assistance in their directions, but even if none do, the follow-up discussion might mention such a possibility, and the usefulness of including the following items:

> lists of items needed to play the game, make the sandwich, or perform the experiment
>
> graphic aids, such as indenting, numbering, drawing lines around important information, and the use of "bullets" to emphasize information
>
> illustrations of a hand performing the card trick; or a line designating the wall for the penny pitching; or the size beakers needed for an experiment
>
> hints on how to hold the cards, win the games, pour the chemicals

Audiences beyond the Classroom

The audience considered in the previous section consisted chiefly of class members, a group towards which student writers could aim merely by being aware of themselves and their own abilities in understanding written material. Target audiences of the following exercises will require more careful examination, for they consist of groups or individuals whom most beginning writers have probably not yet had reason to meet or even consider. These audiences exist in business and industry.

An Exercise in Audience Analysis

This inclass assignment can be accomplished in one class period, is excellent for small group work, and could be used as prewriting work before a longer assignment, such as the analysis of a periodical.

> Directions: (1) What kind of person (educational level, personal interests, motivation, etc.) would enjoy reading each of these three example selections? Be as specific as you can. (2) What characteristics in the selection led you to this view? (3) Choose one of the selections and rewrite it for a different audience.

Example A

Voyager Camera Transmissions from Saturn

On day 1460 (November 12) at 00:52:33 GMT, camera transmissions from Voyager 1 were received at the Deep Space Network sites in Canberra, Australia and Madrid, Spain; high resolution photos from these transmissions were compiled by an ARC 9000 computer at the Jet Propulsion Laboratory in Pasadena, California. Voyager's proximity of 124,240 km from Saturn afforded 487 complete video transmissions of outstanding quality, and when studied by JPL scientists should reveal extensive details of the planet's gaseous core.

Example B

Space Explorer Discovers Icy World

Voyages to the Stars

Voyager I Visits Saturn

As Voyager I plunged onward through the silent blackness of space, scientists and space engineers on Earth stood in wonderment before their complex sensing instruments millions of miles away. They were transfixed by the immensity of what they and the tiny space craft had accomplished.

Suddenly the scientists' video screens flickered again as Voyager's television eye focused on Saturn's lifeless moons, arcing gracefully, along with billions of ice chunks and assorted space debris, across the face of this giant planet. The Earthship quickly began transforming this wondrous picture into electrical impulses and transmitting them back to its distant home planet.

Soon afterward, Voyager's camera motors whirred again, focusing its lenses on the greatest marvel of the spaceship's two year journey. Earth-bound watchers prepared to see their first close-up of Saturn's concentric circles, a wonder of our solar system that has fascinated humans since the invention of the telescope.

Example C

Profits in Space

Will Space Produce the Rich Markets That Will Be Industry's Greatest Challenge?

In your mind, picture giant space vehicles moving effortlessly through the voids of nothingness between planets, delivering precious cargoes of minerals needed for building space platforms and factories on other planets.

This may sound like science fiction, but in Atlanta last week a mixture of governmental officials, military, and industrial leaders met in the beautiful downtown civic auditorium to discuss this very subject: mineral exploration in space.

> As North American Aerospace officials looked on, experts spoke
> of the possibility that civilian spacecraft will soon be transporting
> precious minerals between planets. . . .

This assignment shows that writers adjust the scope and delivery
of their material in attracting and sustaining the interest of an audience. Students will discover that subject matter is merely the first of
several elements the writer molds to fit the readers. This exercise works
especially well when small groups are assigned to each excerpt. Afterwards, a spokesperson for each group may list the conclusions on the
board and discuss the group's findings.

Example A. Students discussing Example A may initially overlook
the title's blandness, which indicates that the author did not feel flashy
beginnings were necessary for the technical audience at which this
excerpt is aimed. They will, however, point out the detail (the numbers:
00:52:33, 9000, and 487) and the jargon ("GMT" for Greenwich Mean
Time, "Deep Space Network," "video transmissions," and "JPL" for
Jet Propulsion Laboratory). Someone may point out that the excerpt
contains numerous passive voice constructions ("were received," "were
compiled"), and the instructor might ask someone to rewrite these
sentences in active voice to compare the difference in readability,
clarity, and emphasis. Passive voice is no longer automatically accepted
by editors of scientific periodicals unless the writer wishes the sentence
to emphasize the object rather than the subject.

Example B. Perhaps the most notable feature of Example B is the
use of drama promoted by the expressive verbs, adjectives, and adverbs:
"plunged," "blackness," "wonderment," "complex," "transfixed," and
so on. The author of this article wants the readers to imagine themselves participating in the event, moving along with Voyager I to
Saturn and seeing what it sees. The breathless prose style is another
feature. Some students may be annoyed at the "Soap-opera" quality of
this excerpt, with all of the action occurring at the peak of emotion.
The titles, similarly, look as if they were on movie marquees. That
there are two indicates the author is not neglecting any possibility
for attracting the audience's attention. Unlike Example A, this article
has a simple sentence structure, and short, journalistic paragraphs with
virtually no complexity or major demands on the reader.

Example C. This final excerpt is similar to B: they both share the
sense of narrative and drama. It begins with a rhetorical question for
its title and contains, as the lead paragraph, a visually appealing
hypothetical scene of space travel. Readability is augmented by short
paragraphs common to journalism. This article is easily visualized
through its use of colorful images like "giant space vehicles" and
"precious cargoes." The target audience may be ascertained from

several key phrases. "Rich markets" and "Industry's Greatest Challenge" imply that this article is for businessmen or stock holders, individuals who find excitement in the challenge of making money in new markets.

This discussion is by no means exhaustive, and students have other elements to point out. Certainly an explanation of why certain excerpts appeal more to them than others could be useful in understanding audience. The following is a brief list of possible areas the class might consider.

Titles: snappy, melodramatic, or restrained

Sentences: lengthy or short, periodic or standard

Tone: dramatic or subdued

Format: amount of "white space"—areas without printing, such as frequent paragraph indentations and wide margins (Extensive white space conveys the impression of something quickly and thus easily read, like a newspaper or popular magazine.)

The three selections should provoke a useful discussion on several major points of audience analysis. For example, students should realize that the same subjects are often described in diverse ways, according to the needs of the particular audience, and that successful writers must be skilled in understanding these various readers. Continuing this point, the class might discuss what magazines would print each of the excerpts. If, say, *Scientific American* printed an article on the exploration of Saturn, how would it deal with the subject differently than *Popular Science*? Such a discussion would be particularly useful before the class turns to an analysis of periodicals, for the excerpts should prepare students to analyze writing style in determining audience.

Audiences of Periodicals

Magazine or journal analysis is a useful assignment for everyone, because nearly all disciplines report information to the public through such media. This assignment shows that professional writers must carefully consider their audiences before composing.

The class should have access to several magazines which address special groups, such as certain hobbyists, age groups, or academic areas. While in small groups, the students identify the audience of the periodicals they have been assigned and what features led them to this conclusion:

the various advertisements for special products

topics discussed in the articles

formatting—whether conservative and restrained like *The New Yorker* or flashy like *People* magazine

the editor's requirements for submitted articles—topics considered or encouraged; manuscript length and style sheet to follow; use of photographs

indication of whether the editor or outside referees decide on acceptance or rejection of the manuscript, and how long this decision normally takes

A student or the teacher should list the conclusions on the board, after which students are asked to write an analysis of a periodical of their choice, selecting one or two representative elements from the magazine (advertisements, format, etc.) and describing the audience to whom these appeal.

Audiences in the Business World

Business communication is much concerned with audience analysis, whether it involves reports, letters, or memos. Writers at the various levels of business organizations always consider who may read the correspondence; often their success or failure depends on their ability to skillfully analyze and write towards a particular audience. Students can be given experience with the conventions of business communication—especially its concern with audience—by combining letter-writing assignments with the case method.

The case method was developed in business and law schools to present students with actual situations and allow them to contemplate the evidence and circumstances, as did the original attorneys or businessmen. This method now frequently appears in classrooms of various disciplines, and it can be used quite effectively to teach audience. The cases may be simple or complex, depending upon the skill level of the class and the time allotted to the assignment.[8]

Letter-writing assignments often provide students with a practical look into the work world. Because they are relatively short yet significant pieces of communication, letters work well in the classroom. Generally, these assignments are more realistic if the instructor does not read the problem, but rather distributes some form of written communication to which the students respond.

In the periodical audience exercise, the students visualized an audience (probably without realizing it) and tried to reconstruct an author's subconscious reasoning while composing for a specific audience. In this next exercise, however, the students themselves attempt to determine how their audience may be best addressed and where their audience is open to persuasion.

Negotiating by Letter

> After several days you and your wife found a home you liked and could afford, although barely. You painstakingly determined the maximum monthly payment you could pay, and located a bank which would give you mortgage money at 11.5 percent. You return to your older home and get ready to move when the following letter arrives from the lending bank. Write a letter in response.

May 22, 1981

Mr. and Mrs. Paul O'Hara
209 Spring Valley Road
Columbia, MO 65201

Dear Mr. and Mrs. O'Hara:

> The Copper Country Bank is pleased to offer you a commitment in the amount of $25,500 for a term of twenty (20) years at an interest rate of 11.75 percent.

> I have heard that you have already taken care of the property insurance with a local agent. As you know, the amount we require must cover the loan proceeds and show us as the mortgagee, which you have done. With reference to the loan rate, you will note that it is a quarter percent above what we discussed at the time of the application. During the time we were underwriting the loan and prior to our commitment, our rates did increase. The new payment is on the enclosed Real Estate Mortgage Loan Disclosure Statement. I hope this does not inconvenience you.

> Thank you for your interest in the Copper Country Bank, and we look forward to seeing you in the future.

Very truly yours,

J.W. Logan

John W. Logan
Branch Manager
Copper Country Bank
Houghton, MI 49931

If the class knows little of letter-writing skills (format and structure) further class discussion on Logan's letter could prove useful. In business writing, Logan's correspondence would be called a "Bad News Letter." He has bad news to present, and, of course, wants to give it as painlessly as possible. How is this done? Bad news is least upsetting when it is deemphasized, so Logan begins his letter with the *good* news that the loan has been approved. One can sense the drama of the first line, almost as if it were accompanied by fanfare: "The Copper Country Bank is pleased to offer. . . ." Logan temporarily continues with good news into paragraph two by referring to the insurance requirement being fulfilled. While this information isn't as exciting, it may be legally necessary, and it certainly is not disappointing. However, after we are lulled into believing that life is worth living and God is on our side, we are presented with the bad news. This begins very innocently with the phrase: "With reference to," a vague, colorless group of words common to legal documents—Logan is retreating into business jargon. The bad news has not only been held until the middle of the letter, it is further embedded in a weak part of the sentence.[9]

To prepare the class for writing the response, prewriting techniques might include class discussion and a journal write. General class discussion will clear up any confusion the students may have about the problem the bank's letter poses—how to talk Logan into returning the interest rate to the previously agreed level. A journal write or small group discussion will assist the students in considering arguments that might change Logan's mind. They should consider where a bank is vulnerable; in other words, what is the major concern of such an institution besides being profitable? One possible approach: the bank's reputation for honesty and fairness.

Finally, the students must consider how to structure their response. Should they also write their letter with the bad news embedded, or should they place their irritation in a more forceful position? Here is a sample response:

209 Spring Valley Road
Columbia, MO 65201
May 25, 1981

Mr. John W. Logan, Manager
Copper Country Bank
Houghton, MI 49931

Dear Mr. Logan:

I wish to thank you for informing us that our loan application has been approved.

However, my wife and I are upset and confused by the notification that our interest rate has been raised from that agreed upon in your office a few weeks ago. During our short visit to Michigan in early April we contacted several lending institutions and decided upon Copper Country Bank, both for its competitive loan rate and its reputation among our new acquaintances in the area. I talked over the telephone with a Copper Country loan officer, and he double checked on the interest rate. He assured me that the current rate for such a loan was 11.5 percent. My wife and I later drove to your bank and discussed this rate. The legal papers you gave us at that time specifies the lower interest rate. Thus I am surprised that Copper Country would raise the interest rate after we left the area and returned to Missouri.

If a bank can do this, how does a customer determine whether information received from bank officials is valid or not? Your letter states that the bank had not yet made a "commitment." Certainly the commitment to grant us the loan had not been made, for the bank must check our credit references; but we accepted the information given us for the interest rate, and that commitment, I believe, should be upheld.

My family and I are presently 900 miles from the Copper Country Bank, and are thus in no position to negotiate a new loan with another lending institution. Nor do we wish to do so. Therefore, I am asking Copper Country Bank to reconsider and loan the mortgage funds at the interest rate specified when the application was made three weeks ago. We are looking forward to our new home in Michigan and hope that our dealings with one of the area's leading banking institutions does not begin with this unfortunate situation.

Please let us hear from you soon about this matter.

Sincerely,

Paul O'Hara

Paul O'Hara

Unlike Logan's letter, O'Hara's response is more forward. The author felt that one of his major weapons was anger, and thus he states in a prominent place that he is disappointed that the interest rate was changed. He didn't, however, wish the bank to forget about the loan entirely, for he was several hundred miles away and couldn't easily find another bank. Besides, the other banks wanted even higher interest rates (if not, he would have dealt with them to begin with). Therefore he began and concluded the letter by mentioning that he did not want to change lending institutions.

The second major argument in this letter is that the bank's action is unfair. The majority of the copy is directed at this point: building up the case against changing the rate. If such things can be done, the author asks, how can anyone do business? Note that the letter lacks hostility; rather than empty rhetoric and threats, the letter makes its point with detail—a step by step record of the transaction and why the O'Hara's were surprised at the change in interest rates.

The letter concludes with images of what all banks hope to be in the community—pillars of honesty. Of course the implication here is that if the bank does not change the interest rate then they do not fit into the appropriate pattern of honesty.

Advocacy with Diverse Audiences

A colleague provided me with the following example.[10] It can be completed in one class period and calls for addressing several different audiences. The class should be broken into groups of five.

> For several days rumors have been reported that federal and state authorities are considering the construction of a nuclear

power plant five miles north of town on the Eagle River. Each member of the group is to compose a response to this planned construction, directing the communication to one of the five audiences listed below (be sure that all five audiences are covered).

The self (as if in a journal)

A close and trusted friend

A teacher in a physics class who has asked you to discuss the advantages and/or disadvantages of such a project

A large, unknown audience, such as the readers of a locally published magazine or newspaper Sunday supplement

The governor of our state

Try to write one or two substantial paragraphs. You have about fifteen minutes to do this piece of writing.

After completing the writing, students identify their target audiences and read their material to other members of their group. Then group members discuss the differences of each piece of communication, noting how the different audiences produced different problems and how each writer attempted to solve them.

Here are student examples which resulted from this exercise in a freshman level composition class.

Journal Entry

I just heard they're building a nuke plant north of town. I hope it gets inspected well, is built far enough away so that if it explodes the dorm is still standing, and that the wind starts blowing to the north. At least we'll have some dependable power for once. I wonder how I'd look as a mutant?

This example shows a typical style of writing common to journals: although the first line establishes the subject, the paragraph has no formal beginning or end. Instead, each idea is discussed in the order the writer's mind becomes aware of it—in an informal, meandering way. He begins with an allusion to the power plant's danger, and worries about it exploding the dorm; then he shifts to a more positive view that it could provide dependable power, but then returns to the negative by mentioning the possibility of being a mutant. The paragraph also contains humor, and it assumes certain knowledge by the reader (himself), such as that he lives in a dorm. The perspective is from someone who has an interest in the subject but has not yet taken a stand for or against.

A Close Friend

Dear Nancy,

Have you heard the rumors about the Nuclear Power Plant that is being built in Eagle River? I shouldn't say it is, because I don't know for sure. I don't think it will ever go through though because too many people will protest the idea. No one will want a power plant in this area. Personally, I am against it because of the imperfections of the plants.

If you hear anything about it let me know, I am very interested.

Sincerely yours,

Terri

Terri

Terri has written a slightly more formal piece of communication than the journal, but there are also many similarities. Like the journal, Terri's letter also makes assumptions about what her audience knows: for example, Nancy knows who Terri is and that an introduction is not necessary. The writing style is relaxed, and dusted with conversational phrases, such as "I don't know for sure," and "if you hear anything. . . ." Like the journal, her letter begins with a sentence establishing the topic, but instead of moving from one side of the issue to the other, her message supports a single view. The format is also different, for Terri has selected the more formal structure of correspondence, with a salutation and complimentary close. Some students might realize that the audience for a letter demands some logical structure and could be confused by the meanderings of someone's journal.

Physics Teacher

The possibility of a nuclear plant being built in the area has some advantages. The nuclear plant will be able to supply the area with power at a low cost with a resource that is in relative abundance. The reactor will produce power with no real air pollution. Also, the nuclear plant will have little effect on the forests and the creatures around it.

However, the cooling water of the plant could have a slight effect on the surrounding water if it is put back at too high a temperature. It may raise the water temperature too much and kill off the species of fish and plants. Also, the slight possibility of a nuclear spill could affect the wildlife if it was large.

This student made certain assumptions about his audience that are different from the previous writings. Although the directions indicated that the physics teacher would accept either advantages or disadvantages, this student felt that a science teacher would consider both sides. The formality is greater in this selection. There is no reference to human beings reading the material, and no reference to how the plant has the potential for harm to humans; instead, the author stresses the negative in terms of the environment and fish.

Unknown Audience—Newspaper

It has come to my attention that a nuclear power plant has been proposed for an area north of town on the Eagle River. A rumor has spread that state and federal authorities are backing this issue. While no official word is out on this matter, my sources seem to agree that this rumor is true. No word has been given as to which town on the Eagle River has been chosen as the site of the proposed plant. The construction of a nuclear plant has always been a controversial matter, and this paper will cover both sides of this issue as it develops.

This student writer may be aware that an editorial should take a stand on an issue, but he may not be sure which side to support; therefore, he takes neither, promising instead that the paper will cover both sides in future issues. The author wants to provide as many specific details as possible, but he also senses that a newspaper should be objective and accurate, so he covers possible errors with vagueness: "a rumor has spread that . . ." and "while no official word is out." For style, this author knows that editorials are generally more formal than journals and friendly letters, and probably feels that this sense of formality can be communicated with the passive voice: "It has come to my attention," and "No word has been given."

The Governor of the State of Michigan
Governor Milliken:
    I have heard a rumor that the state and federal governments are thinking about putting a nuclear power plant in this area on Eagle River. I feel that this is a tremendous idea and that it would help the economy in this area a great deal. Not only would it provide jobs for hundreds or thousands of people, but it would also help this area come out of the past and move into the future.
    I am sure that many people will disagree with this thinking but the economy is what must be thought of and nuclear power, I feel, is one of the answers.

This response is similar to an editorial in that it takes a strong stand on an issue. The writer is more highly aware of audience than the previous examples, for he refers to at least two audiences: the governor, when mentioning the economic advantages to the state (information that presumably would motivate a politician), and the opposition (to the author's view), "many people will disagree with this thinking but. . . ."

To complete the assignment, the instructor makes five columns on the board, corresponding to each audience. The students then explain what formats, word choices, and tone they used in their paragraphs. The result shows the spectrum from expressive to transactional writing: from the relaxed, less inhibited characteristics of expressive writing, to the more formal, restrained tone and delivery of the transactional communication written for a general audience.

Conclusion

In our discussion of audience we considered a fifteen-year-old high school student testing jokes on his class, not realizing that he had, in the process, actually performed a complex though mistaken analysis of audience. One of the guiding principles of this chapter's discussion is that beginning writers, like the joke-teller, have an incipient under-standing of audience, but they are unaware of how to use this knowl-edge when writing. This chapter has offered a method which guides writers through a series of classroom assignments, each demanding a more complex analysis of the readers. Students are thus guided from their intuitive understanding of audience to the complex demands of written discourse in the adult world. While audience is only one of many elements to consider when communicating, it is certainly one of the most important.

Notes

1. Maxine Hairston, *A Contemporary Rhetoric,* 2nd ed. (Boston: Houghton Mifflin, 1978), p. 107. James Britton also writes of this distinction between oral and written audience analysis. See James Britton, Tony Burgess, Nancy Martin, Alex McLeod, and Harold Rosen, *The Development of Writing Abilities (11–18)* (London: Macmillan Education, 1975), p. 58.

2. For a review of audience as taught in composition texts, see Lisa S. Ede, "On Audience and Composition," *College Composition and Communication* 30 (October 1979): 291–295.

3. Britton, pp. 68–73.

4. Britton, p. 122.

5. See Barry Kroll, "Cognitive Egocentrism and the Problem of Audience Awareness in Written Discourse," *Research in the Teaching of English* 12 (October 1978): 269–281. However, not every student whose writing neglects audience is necessarily egocentric. Fred R. Pfister and Joanne F. Petrick, in their essay, "A Heuristic Model for Creating a Writer's Audience," *College Composition and Communication* 30 (May 1980): 213–220, incorrectly label some of their students egocentric who "were so worried about getting down on paper what they had to say that they could not be bothered worrying about anyone else's response to their writing." Such individuals do not match Moffett's definition of the problem; rather, these students may well know the importance of audience but are unable to move beyond preliminary communication blocks, such as word selection. Because they lack the most basic word skills, they are unable to move on to later, more sophisticated steps like audience analysis.

6. James Moffett, *Teaching the Universe of Discourse* (Boston: Houghton Mifflin, 1968), p. 195.

7. While I have changed most of these questions, I am indebted for the initial concept to Pfister and Petrick's "A Heuristic Model for Creating a

Writer's Audience," *College Composition and Communication* 30 (May 1980): 213–220.

8. For textbooks using the case method, see John P. Field and Robert H. Weiss, *Cases for Composition* (Boston: Little, Brown, 1979); and David Tedlock and Paul Jarvie, *Casebook Rhetoric: A Problem-Solving Approach to Composition* (New York: Holt, Rinehart and Winston, 1981). The text by Field and Weiss consists almost entirely of short, narrative cases, while the book by Tedlock and Jarvie, as their title suggests, also offers rhetorical methodology. Another distinction is in the types of cases. The latter book deals with more controversial issues, such as premarital sexual relations and gay rights.

9. A writer may emphasize or deemphasize ideas according to where they are placed in a sentence. When placed at the beginning or end of a sentence, key words communicate more vividly to the reader. This concept is easily proven by considering the trick question "How many animals did Moses take with him aboard the Ark?" The answer, of course, is that Noah, not Moses boarded the Ark. People are often fooled by this because the key word, "Moses," is placed in that part of the sentence which is least effective for conveying important information: the middle. The misleading terms "animals" and "Ark" occupy the more effective sections of the sentence, the beginning and end.

10. For this assignment I am indebted to Randall R. Freisinger, "James Britton and the Importance of Audience," *English Language Arts Bulletin* 20/21 (Winter/Spring 1980): 5–8.

6 Considering Values: The Poetic Function of Language

Art Young
Michigan Technological University

"When did you first realize that you wanted to become a poet?"
My question is "when did other people give up the idea of being a
poet?" You know, when we are kids we make up things, we write,
and for me the puzzle is not that some people are still writing, the
real question is why did the other people stop?

William Stafford
Writing the Australian Crawl

Somewhere along the line, I think about sixth grade, our system of
mass education gives up on creative writing as a useful learning experience. The rationale seems to be that true proficiency in creative
writing is a gift from the gods given to the inspired few who are pre-
destined to become great artists no matter what their educational experience, and that further opportunities for everyone else to write
poetically serves no useful purpose. Nevertheless, creativity continues
to have eloquent advocates. One of them, Jacob Bronowski, has written
on the motivation, pleasure, creativity, and commitment of both the
scientist and artist at work. His representation of the individual's
unique sense of self when exploring for new knowledge, whether in
science or art, should be experienced by students in all disciplines.

> The need of the age gives its shape to scientific progress as a whole.
> But it is not the need of the age which gives the individual scientist
> his sense of pleasure and excitement which keeps him working late
> into the night when all the useful typists have gone home at five
> o'clock. He is personally involved in his work, as the poet in his,
> as the artist is in the painting. Paints and painting too must have
> been made for useful ends, and language was developed, from
> whatever beginnings, for practical communication. Yet you cannot
> have a man handle paints or language or the symbolic concepts
> of physics, you cannot even have him stain a microscopic slide,
> without instantly waking in him a pleasure in the very language,
> a sense of exploring his own activity. This sense lies at the heart of
> creation.[1]

Creative writing is one important way to wake in a student "a pleasure in the very language, a sense of exploring his own activity," and this can be done in science, humanities, business, or engineering courses. We are familiar with testimonials from many sources which acknowledge that the creative impulse is central to the development, understanding, and application of knowledge. Reasoning by analogy and communicating by metaphor are generally recognized as integral strategies of successful thinkers and writers in every discipline.

This chapter describes ways that the poetic function of language can be used to develop students' abilities to learn and write in any field of study. In Nancy Martin's words:

> We wouldn't claim to understand fully what happens when children's imagination is brought into play, but in its widest sense we would regard imagination as that mental process which enables a person to make his own connections, whether this happens to be in the sciences or in the arts. It may be that those moments are rare when an "imaginative leap" opens up new patterns and new perspectives for others, but unless we provide many opportunities all over the curriculum for children to use their imaginations more extensively, their knowledge will remain inert.[2]

Most teachers, regardless of grade level, would like students to use their imaginations and make personal value assessments when learning new materials. James Britton puts it this way:

> As the stories children write (whether autobiographical or fictional) become "shaped stories," more art-like, they move from Expressive towards the Poetic. The more "shaped" they become, the more effectively they enable writers to explore and express their *values,* those ways of feeling and believing about the world that make us the sorts of people we are.[3]

The poetic function of written language becomes important when individuals attempt to relate new knowledge to their value systems. People use language poetically to serve a wide variety of functions in their lives; this chapter explains how poetic language helps students assess knowledge in terms of their own systems of beliefs. Poetic writing in its most familiar and completed forms is what most of us would recognize as, among other things, poetry, stories, plays, and parables. All teachers, of course, need not become creative writing teachers in some formal sense, but teachers from all disciplines can elicit creative language—and thus creative thinking—from students. All functions of language assist in shaping our beliefs, but poetic language especially helps us understand the now familiar dicta from physics and poetry that one cannot separate the observer from the observed, the dancer from the dance.

Characteristics of the Poetic

To return for a moment to the theoretical model discussed earlier in this book, James Britton asserts that written language begins in the *expressive* and then moves outward from the self along a continuum toward either *transactional or poetic.*[4] (See Figure 1.) The purpose of language

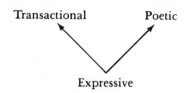

Figure 1.

which moves along the continuum from expressive to transactional language is to get things done. The purpose of language which moves along the continuum from expressive to poetic is to develop and examine knowledge in the light of one's own value system—poetic language is important *for its own sake.* With expressive language as the base, both transactional and poetic language should be effective capacities of every individual—one taps the gift of reason and one the gift of imagination—and both gifts can be developed by using written language. Figure 2 offers a more elaborate diagram.

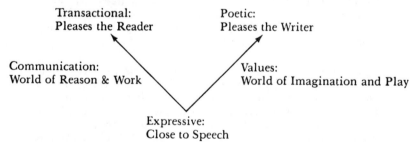

Figure 2.

Expressive to Poetic

In cases where the writing tends to the poetic but is not "shaped," we recognize the poetic by writing's function rather than by its form. Such writing occurs at an intermediary point along Britton's expressive-poetic continuum, where form may not be very well developed, but function—to evaluate new experience in the light of past experience—can be very significant pedagogically (Figure 3). By way of illustration consider two short informal paragraphs in which American Literature

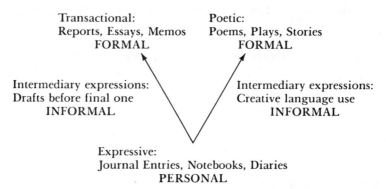

Figure 3.

students evaluate Emily Dickinson's relationship with nature in terms of their own understanding of nature.

> Being a satisfied disciple of Jesus Christ, I disagree with the importance Emily places on nature. She sees nature as a parent and the rest of the world under her care. Humans were never intended to be "mothered" by nature. Instead, as according to Genesis 1:26, God placed human life above every other lifeform (Then God said, "Let us make a man—someone like ourselves, to be the master of all life upon the earth and in the skies and in the seas"). According to this, I believe man has total power over nature in that he can use it in any way he can and sees fit.

> They had a moral code. Now I understand, mind you, that some people rebelled against it, but at least there was something to rebel *against*. They knew where they were, and so the courageous ones could strike out on their own, *from* someplace *to* someplace. They had a culture. We either don't have one or have one too embarrassing to admit to. I can never decide which. I think maybe I'm just writing this on a bad day, because even tho I'm no Puritan, I think I would rather be there than here. The only thing this has to do with Emily D. is that I started feeling this way reading her letters.

These students are making connections in writing between themselves and what they are learning—making connections between the subject matter of the course and their own feelings and beliefs.

Personal Knowledge

New knowledge always confronts an individual's value system. The knowledge might be *dismissed* as inaccurate or irrelevant because the individual cannot cope with its validity and maintain some value system; the knowledge might be *assimilated* and radically alter an individual's value system by challenging and changing its assumptions at the core; or the knowledge might interact significantly with the individual's value system and be *accommodated* as enriching or refining the individual's value system. After students have reacted personally in writing to the material, opportunities for further study should be provided—to analyze, synthesize, verify or dismiss, assimilate, accommodate. In the student examples above, such study might focus on the nineteenth-century transcendentalism/fundamentalism debate, the protestant work ethic in American culture—then and now, the contemporary environmentalist/developer controversies, or further study of nature in the works of Emily Dickinson and other American writers, such as Emerson, Whitman, and Melville.

Unless students tune-out, or play the game of giving the teacher only what they assume the teacher wants to hear, students respond to what we teach by making knowledge meaningful to themselves or—as they often say in their writings—by discovering how they "feel" about it. When students explore this process in writing, they produce a document which they can assess in terms of personal values and which, in conjunction with other written assessments, provides visual access to self-knowledge—a traditional goal of liberal education. Teachers can use this kind of student writing to make the content of the course—whether American literature, economic history, or Cartesian philosophy—accessible and meaningful to students. As students grow in knowledge, they should be encouraged to make it personal and thereby grow in understanding and responsibility—in one sense *the final test* of a purposeful and humane education.

The Self-Conscious Question

In addition to asking students to relate class material to personal concerns, a teacher can ask students to write informally in preparation for a formal assignment (whether an essay, a lab report, a reading assignment, or an objective test). Janet Emig, in her analysis of the composing process of student writers, notes the kinds of things students think about as they write, but also notes the things they never appear to think about. At no time does any of the students ask aloud any variants of the questions: "Is this subject important to me?" "Do I care about writing about it?"[5] Such questions make excellent expressive → poetic writing assignments in any class.

> Why should I study microbiology?
> Is European literature important to me?
> What did I learn from today's lecture on Jeffersonian democracy?
> Am I interested in doing a case study for Personal Finance?
> How is writing this forestry paper going to help me be a forester?
> Why do teachers make us write all the time?

Such questions, when asked aloud and then responded to in writing (and class discussion), diminish the alienation of classroom assignments from the student's own sense of purpose and motivation.

Student Examples

Below are passages from two students who were asked to respond briefly (in class) to the question: Why write a formal (transactional) paper on a work of literature?

> By writing a formal paper, you want to get an idea across clearly, neatly, and concisely. You want your reader to be able to go through it and understand immediately what you are saying without having them stop and ask questions—about your purpose or grammar and spelling mistakes. You write a formal paper to make sure you don't make mistakes, to make sure you're organized, and to make sure you don't leave anything out, by using an outline, a rough draft, and proofreading.

> Writing a formal paper on a literary topic helps the student to understand what the author is trying to get across. When I sat down to write about the poems of e. e. cummings, I did not really understand his poetry in the least. But when I started to write, the process of putting the words down on paper opened up the poems. I think that English teachers know that the student tends to read and not comprehend what he is reading. By making the student write an assignment on the whole or a specific aspect of a literary work, the teacher is doing the student a great service. The same is true of any subject, even "Why do you write a formal paper." It forces the student to think about what he is doing, and in the process sets off a chain reaction of thinking about the subject and things related to the subject.

Students write for a variety of reasons—and to please the teacher is among the most important to them. In asking students to evaluate various assignments, written or otherwise, and to do such a task *for its own sake* is to provide them with the opportunity to discriminate among the different functions of language, to confront the personal as well as the social significance of the material they are asked to learn, to recognize distinctions between exterior restraints (to please a reader) and interior motivation (to comprehend and communicate knowledge), to use written language to make connections and imagine possibilities, and to discover and communicate specific information.

Forms of the Poetic

Thus far I have discussed the function of poetic writing when it is close to the expressive, that is when the form—perhaps informal essays and journal entries—is related only to the student, and learning, imagining, and evaluating (dismissing, assimilating, accommodating) are unencumbered by the demands of rhetorical purpose and an expectant audience. Further along the continuum from self-expressive language to the more formally poetic, form becomes important. The experience of writing in poetic form transforms thought and assists the writer in achieving the personal (evaluating new experience) and social (imaginative empathy and insight) purposes of the poetic.

The familiar forms of stories, plays, poems, as well as numerous other forms of the poetic are readily available for classroom use; examples include monologs, dialogs, role-playing scenarios, interviews, scripts, aphorisms, epigrams, parables, and fictive or dramatic techniques applied to traditional transactional forms: case studies, letters, informative reports, and persuasive essays. The process of writing to the demands of poetic form alters expression of content and produces new perceptions of experience, which in turn provides the necessary distance for the individual involved in the self-examination of values.

The Writer's Stance and Distance

Poetic form creates a sense of distance. Its distinctive function as a learning tool is to draw the writer into a different role or stance. Transactional writing accomplishes something else—persuades, informs, deceives, or whatever—and in this sense commits the writer to the role of *participant* in the action with a demonstrable stake in its success. Poetic writing exists for its own sake—to please, reveal, be—and in this sense the writer's stance is as a *spectator* within the active process of creation.[6] Figure 4 offers another perspective on our diagram.

Participant writing involves a self-interested part of the writer attempting to accomplish an actual task in a limited world (a lab report, an environmental-impact statement). Spectator writing involves the whole writer attempting to imagine his total world in response to new

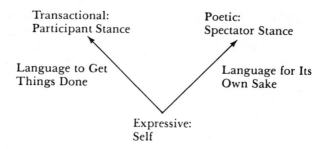

Figure 4.

experience (reading the *Communist Manifesto* or doing a problem in quantum mechanics). Poetic writing pleases and surprises—it is a place for play, imaginative thinking, developing personal knowledge. In its creation it places form above self and in this sense the writer is a spectator.

The spectator stance in poetic writing engages the writer's values. Thus while we say that for the writer poetic writing exists for its own sake, it also serves social and pedagogical purposes in the community and the classroom by developing access to and understanding of value-related activities. We must take pleasure (the poetic) in our purpose (the transactional), that is, make purpose right with the self by understanding the value implications of our actions and beliefs. The poetic function of language provides this distinctive way of assessing experience. As James Britton says, poetic language is the language of being and becoming.

Student Examples

My experience convinces me that students value poetic language and can recognize and articulate the characteristics of the poetic writing experience. What follows are representative excerpts from freshman students, all majoring in science, business, and engineering. They were asked to evaluate the experience of writing four "imaginative writes" during a literature course in which they also wrote various expressive and transactional pieces. Three of the imaginative writes were related to the novels they read: (1) a monolog from the point of view of a particularly obnoxious character; (2) a dialog by two characters which takes place five years after the novel ends; and (3) a brief story focusing on one character in a man/woman situation. The fourth assignment was a poem on a topic and in a style of their choice. The informal responses were done in class in about fifteen minutes; no discussion regarding the purpose of "imaginative writes" preceded the writing of these responses.

The imaginative writes that we have done for this class have been interesting and fun. They also have taught how to express ideas in an enjoyable way. . . . Most of the time I surprise myself along the way. It is interesting to see how my mind develops an idea to a point I haven't planned. It is more fun to try to please someone than to inform them. By being more fun it is easier than formal prose. Imaginative writing develops the creativity of the writer. This is still another way of developing different points of view.

I think that I actually do enjoy creative writing and just the opportunity to be able to have anything you want happen to the characters. It is true that I actually tend to depict them pretty much as before but I still get the chance to see what it is like to be an author. That provides me with more motivation to do the other assignments. Looking back just now, I realize that when I have some character do something it is most likely to be in the manner in which I see that group in which the person can be classified. That is, I have women doing what I see as the role of women, doctors doing what I see as the role of doctors, etc. I suppose that that is, actually, an indication as to what I am like, believe and see as important. Probably a useful self analysis.

I really enjoyed the writing we've done that was imaginary and you had to interpret actions and characters yourself. I did *no* creative writing in high school and it was really fun to express my feelings and ideas without worrying about a grade or grammar. I enjoyed writing the poem, just to know I could write one and be a little creative. I felt that in the poem and the other imaginative ones, I was expressing more of myself and my feelings than in the other writing assignments we've done. Pretending to be a character and think and act for them also helped define exactly how I viewed them and their relationship in the novel.

I get a pretty neat feeling when I write imaginative essays. I feel in control. I can make the story take any turn I want to. For instance, I didn't like the idea of Anita and Shepherd hitting it off great, so in my essay I decided to write that they were having marital problems. I felt great because I had the chance to express my ideas of what the book should have in it. In real life you have to accept the past the way it was. You can't go around changing it to suit your life. But when I write these essays I have the freedom to change anything. I can write anything I want and know that there is no right or wrong answer.

From the students' point of view poetic writing is valuable for its own sake. Poetic writing *on the subject matter of the class* (in this case, literature) is a unique kind of composing which demands a different stance from the writer toward language, experience, audience, and subject matter. It involves different emotional sensibilities and cognitive operations; and it provides the freedom important to making imaginative connections and realizing values. It also shares with expressive and transactional writing the function of enabling students to better understand course material they are studying.

Most of my students write many more words in their imaginative writes than in their formal ones, and yet many feel a little guilty because it is so easy and so much fun. Most students spend many hours working on these "easy" and "enjoyable" assignments. Creative writing exercises in nonwriting classes may produce surprise or even bewilderment among students, but they should have the opportunity to use the poetic function of writing throughout their education.

Classroom Exercises.

Here are some examples of poetic writing exercises that will enable students to reflect on the subject matter of the course.

Informal, imaginative essays. Such assignments encourage students to develop and clarify their personal value systems in response to course material. Possibilities include: (1) the "What if . . ." assignment (What if a four-lane highway were built in a specific rural area? What if the A-bomb had not been dropped on Hiroshima and Nagasaki as the way to end World War II?); (2) the "I feel . . ." assignment (I feel American race relations could be eased by . . . , I feel the computer industry will . . .); and (3) the "Value of . . ." assignment (the value of the engineer's professional code is . . . , the value of anti-trust legislation is . . . , the value of Picasso's work is . . .).

Role-playing. These exercises ask students to imagine, dramatically, how they would behave or what they would do in specified situations, past, present, or future. Some examples include: (1) for a marketing class—write a descriptive scenario from the point of view of a senior citizen shopping at a local grocery store; (2) for an anthropology class—consider from the point of view of a Laplander your new ownership of a snowmobile; (3) for a political science class—write a series of three monologs on the recent Supreme Court decision on police access to media documents from the point of view of a thankful police officer, a shocked reporter, and a U.S. Senator considering options to mitigate or change the decision; (4) for an American literature class—write a dialog between Emily Dickinson and Walt Whitman discussing the role of nature in their lives; (5) for a philosophy class—compose graffiti ("God is Dead"—Nietzsche, "Nietzsche is Dead"—God); (6) for a mathematics class—interview fellow students on how they solve homework problems and then write brief reports from the interviewees points of view using their exact words wherever possible; and (7) for a nursing class—present a case study of a terminal cancer patient in the year 2000 with specific reference to how death with dignity issues will be handled at that time.

Metaphors and parables. Analogy is widely associated with creative thinking as a way of making knowledge meaningful. These exercises ask students to write about new knowledge in metaphors and parables; they also demonstrate how professionals in specific fields use these language devices in their own writing. The following parable might be distributed in either a science or a humanities class.

The Parable of the Pike

Placed in a tank with some minnows but separated from them by a sheet of glass, the pike bangs its head for some time in an effort to get at them. At length it sensibly gives up the effort. Much less sensibly, it continues to ignore the minnows after the glass is removed; it fails to reevaluate the situation. In other words, it becomes a dogmatist.[7]

Students can write on what the parable says about scientific method and enquiry or about one possible human response to experience. They can write and compare their own imitative parables. They can write a parable about another subject using the pike as a metaphor or something of their own invention. Students in science, engineering, and humanities classes can study in the following passage Albert Einstein's use of metaphoric language to make new knowledge comprehensible and right with the self.

Physical concepts are free creations of the human mind, and are not, however it may seem, uniquely determined by the external world. In our endeavor to understand reality we are somewhat like a man trying to understand the mechanism of a closed watch. He sees the face and the moving hands, even hears its ticking, but he has no way of opening the case. If he is ingenious he may form some picture of a mechanism which could be responsible for all the things he observed, but he may never be quite sure his picture is the only one which could explain his observations. He will never be able to compare his picture with the real mechanism and he cannot even imagine the possibility of the meaning of such a comparison.[8]

Students can write using the metaphor of the watch in many areas of intellectual concern. And when they do, information that is not new to us teachers but is new to our students can be better understood by their relating the new to the familiar. Such exercises provide students with the opportunity to make knowledge their own.

Stories, dramas, poems. These more recognizable forms of the poetic need not be limited to literature classes. Students can be given such assignments with very little preparation, for while most have not written much in these forms in high school or college, in either English or other classes, they "know" how to go about it. Such assignments can be made specific to the course content as well as made more general as exercises in imagination, value assessment, and poetic language. Some examples of specific course-related assignments include: (1) in recreational geography—write a play for campers at a nearby urban park; (2) in genetics—write a story on the cloning of prize beef cattle; (3) in French—write a poem on language and cultural idiosyncrasies; (4) in mechanical engineering—write a short parody of the textbook; and (5) in literature—write an epilogue to *Huckleberry Finn* in which Huck meets up again with Tom Sawyer. In addition to writing assignments that originate with the teacher, students will have appropriate suggestions of their own.

Poetry and Philosophy

In an Introduction to Philosophy class at Michigan Tech, the instructor had assigned the first two "Meditations" by René Descartes for reading and study prior to class discussion. This is a particularly difficult reading assignment for most people, but especially for students without prior experience in philosophy. After the class discussion the teacher assigned a poem to be written on the subject of the two "Meditations." Prior to this assignment students had not written creatively in this class (indeed the teacher had never given creative writing assignments before), and only by chance had they previously read two limericks on Berkeley which were in their textbook. The teacher gave no further instructions except to say that the poem could be in any form and style and would not be graded. When he collected the poems later in the week he asked each student to write for ten minutes on the experience of writing the poem. Here is a representative sample of the writings.

> Descartes said,
> Do I really have a head?
> Maybe it's a perception
> or possibly a deception.
> Everything I have known
> is somewhat doubtful
> but still, highly probable.
>
> Yet I have shown
> it to be, more reasonable
> to believe than to deny in full.
>
> Some malignant demon
> who is at once exceedingly
> potent and deceitful,

has taken to it ardently
to deceive me in full
and that all things be illusions.

Doubtless, then, I exist
since I am deceived.
And never will I cease to exist
as long as in my mind it is conceived.

What am I?
I'm a thinking thing.
What's a thinking thing?
It's a thing that doubts, affirms and conceives
and it also understands, imagines and perceives
All of these am I.

To look at objects that are known
let's use as example, fresh cut beeswax.
Melt it down, and yet remains beeswax.
Thus it can be shown
that it is an intuition of the mind,
and the same of all its kind.

Thus it is that bodies are perceived
by intellectual thought, and not by sight or touch.
Thus it can be conceived
that it is my mind that does this much.

I thought that writing a poem about Descartes and his meditations
was an interesting way to get through them. It made me go over the
reading more carefully than I had done before, resulting in
catching of a few more points that he had made. Overall I would
say that this experience resulted in a more thorough understanding
and a deeper learning experience on my part.

Existence I Think
Here I sit in thought I ponder
The truth, existence, this I wonder
Are my senses true? I reason—
or illusion, tricks, confusions.
Are there Demons, beings evil
Trick me make me think I'm real
Is this body here I see
Just a vision or is it me?
Can I say I really exist
I need facts, reasons for this!
In my mind I think these thoughts,
For existence so hard I fought
Strike down this demon with a blow
With a Gods unearthly glow
With this God benevolent and kind
I create me in my mind
So conclusions, this I find
I exist—within my mind!

I thought the exercise was interesting because: (1) I had to review the readings; (2) I had to plan the verse I wrote; (3) Word choice was critical; (4) Organization was important and difficult; (5) Do you know of a word that rhymes with reason? Overall I enjoyed the assignment for nonrational reasons!

           Descarte
           Philosopher
           UNSURE
           Questioned
           mind, body
           Statement
       not true if can be false
          Sense Experience
          Cartesian Demon
             Deceived

              SURE
              Exists
    to be deceived have to be here
          Cogito Ergo Sum
            What am I?
            Res Cogitans
           Physical World?
             Bees Wax
            Melt, change
           Still Bees Wax?
               Yes!
          Physical Objects
        Intuition of the Mind!

I thought it was a good idea. Poem writing is difficult for me, but since we could do it any way we wanted it was fun and at the same time it was a good review over Descartes' *Meditations*. It gave me a chance to pick out key points and stress them. I am sure they will stay with me longer. It was a good learner tool, I think you should use it again.

I thought that I would have a beer,
And contemplate if I was here
But then it was reconfirmed,
When I flunked winter term.

Writing this poem was easy and kind of fun.

This brief poetic writing exercise was an important learning experience for many of the students for the following reasons: significant ideas in Descartes' *Meditations* were reread and ordered; students' assessed the study of philosophy in general and Descartes in particular;

"imaginative connections" were made on the subject matter of philosophy; student writers played with language and ideas; metaphor and analogy were used for expression and thought; writing poetry became fun and easy, even though it took time and thought; abstract thought was transformed to personal understanding; new knowledge was shaped in relation to individual feelings and beliefs; speculation occurred about the significance of this learning experience; language and thought were appreciated for their own sake.

At the conclusion of this exercise, the philosophy instructor and I discussed ways in which the value of the exercise might be amplified for the class through oral presentations and discussion within the classroom. I asked the instructor if he would take about twenty minutes and jot down informally his impressions of the assignment. Here is what he wrote.

> I made the poetry writing assignment with considerable trepidation. I expected my students to either not do it, or make a very minimal effort. I also expected them to tell me that writing a poem on Descartes' *Meditations* was the dumbest writing assignment they had ever had.
>
> As far as the learning aspect of the assignment is concerned, I hoped the students would have to reread the *Meditations,* think about the major points Descartes is making in order to pick a "topic" for the poem and, finally, to attempt to better understand one or more of these major points in order to actually write the poem. In brief, I hoped the assignment would force the students to actively seek a better understanding of a difficult philosophical work.
>
> Overall, I am pleased with the way the assignment worked out. Out of thirty-two students, only eight chose not to write a poem. Their reasons were probably varied. Some were absent the day I made the assignment. Some did not think it was worth the effort. The responses of those who did make the effort were almost all positive—indeed, very positive. So much for my fear of my students thinking I was giving them a "dumb" assignment.
>
> I was quite pleased with the poems. While some of them are obviously a rush job, a goodly number show evidence of serious thought. I am convinced that the majority of my students reread the *Meditations* and seriously tried to understand what Descartes is saying. I regard this assignment as a definite pedagogical success. My only reservation about such writing is the propriety of giving students homework which has virtually no impact on their grade.
>
> The assignment produced three surprises for me. The first surprise was the unexpected high number of "good" poems. The second surprise was the enthusiasm of many of the students. The final surprise was the relatively high inverse correlation between students who did well on the poems and those who did well on essay exams.[9]

Responding to the Poetic

When reading and responding to student poetic writings teachers must take their cues from both the purpose of the exercises and the stance of the student writer. The purpose is to relate course material to personal values using poetic language; the stance of the poetic writer is as a spectator. Thus, as students themselves are quick to point out when they write about it, responses from the reader of true or false, right or wrong, good or bad, are not relevant. Readers, including teachers, classmates, and perhaps others, are invited in such writing to share in the writer's experience—the pleasure of the self being and becoming—and they must respect this purpose in the invitation. Poetic writing, as opposed to transactional writing, is not written primarily to please the readers, but the writer. Readers of poetic writing must also adopt a spectator stance (suspend judgment) rather than a partici-pant stance (critical judgment) in order to properly respond to the student's experience. The purpose of poetic writing in subject matter courses is not to teach creative writing or literary analysis, but to provide a unique opportunity for students to engage course material. Needless to say, to formally assign a grade to such writings is an in-appropriate teacher response, and it is for this reason that I label such assignments "informal." Yet we must address the philosophy teacher's concern about the propriety of assigning homework which is not graded. How can a teacher sensibly respond to this particular kind of student writing?

Community Sharing and the Value of Talk

Responses (oral and written) to poetic writing should come from the teacher, from classmates, and from the writer himself. The purposes of such responses should be (1) to increase knowledge about the activity of using poetic language, (2) to provide suggestions for further ex-ploration of course subject matter in relation to the student writer's own values and feelings, and (3) to develop a supportive environment for further growth and development of the students as poetic writers, creative thinkers, and responsible persons. All of the exercises that follow are assigned with the intention that they be shared in the classroom with teachers and fellow students; the students should realize this at the outset. Some students will want to write things they don't wish to share with anyone, or some things they may wish to share with only the teachers. The desire for these kinds of expressive writing experiences should be encouraged, but students should *also* be asked to write what can be and will be shared. The value of talk in this context cannot be underestimated. Classroom talk about student writing provides further opportunity to express, clarify, negotiate, verify, motivate, and "make connections."

Class Exercises

As you read the following descriptions of classroom exercises, you may wish to keep in mind two things: first, a specific example of student poetic writing such as the student poems on Descartes in the preceding section and, second, possible applications to courses in your particular discipline.

> Students in pairs or small groups can exchange their poetic writings and write a response to each author. Teachers need give very little further directions except to set a time limit and mention that the purpose of the response is not to be critical, but personal and supportive.

> Teachers can support the above activity by selecting a poetic writing with student responses to it and sharing them with the entire class on an overhead or opaque projector, on the blackboard, or on dittoed sheets. Questions and comments can be made which increase communal (classroom) understanding of the activity. Students can also make such presentations to the class.

> After students have completed a poetic writing assignment, they can be asked to write a response to the experience of writing it. Students can share their responses in small groups, and the class as a whole can attempt consensus on the value of the particular assignment.

> Teachers can write an assignment along with the students and then share it and their thoughts and feelings about having done it.

> Teachers can provide students with written responses to their poetic writing from various points of view to serve different purposes: (1) teacher as fellow learner—the response is personal and seeks to point out in the student's writing areas of common interest and experience, or the thoughts and feelings it evoked; (2) teacher-student dialog—the response not only makes personal connections to the writing, but encourages further dialog by seeking more information or asking clarifying questions; and (3) teacher as instructor—this response also makes personal connections and offers advice for further study based on the experience shared in the poetic writing, perhaps an article the student might *now* be interested in reading or some suggestions of topics

for formal essays now that the student has demonstrated a personal interest.

Teachers can integrate poetic writing assignments with other reading and writing assignments to make a coherent unit on a particular subject. For example, in a history class students might be asked to write *expressively* in journals about Peter the Great, write *poetically* a short scene of Peter in disguise touring Western Europe, and write *transactionally* an essay about the Westernization of Russia under Peter's rule. Each use of language provides students with the opportunity to assess learning about Peter the Great in a distinct but significant way.

This last coordinated assignment reflects James Britton's suggestion that one kind of writing and thinking (poetic) supports expression in other kinds of language and thought (transactional). As shown in Figure 5, beginning with expressive writing as a base, the writer in

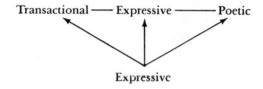

Figure 5.

composing either poetic or transactional writing can draw on the appropriate resources from his experience with the other kind of writing.[10] Thus practice and facility in writing poetically may indeed increase a writer's effectiveness in writing transactionally.

Teacher Response

In our role as evaluators we see that students differ in facility and success when writing a particular poetic assignment. Nevertheless, responding to students' poetic writing is not the time to assume the role of evaluator. Teachers can best help students increase their facility with poetic language by respecting the primary value-related purpose of the poetic, by foregoing traditional formal criticism of the writing, and by employing the variety of collaborative learning experiences outlined in the six suggestions above. By the time many students reach high school and college, the biggest obstacle to writing poetically is convincing themselves that they have some creative talent and that the teacher would like to encourage it—that there is not a hidden agenda lurking beneath the teacher's expression of good will. Many students view *all* assignments as having only one purpose, to be graded according to a formal standard. This purpose, when practiced exclusively, inhibits the use of language for other worthwhile purposes.

Certainly teachers can expect students who wish a satisfactory or good grade in a course to participate fully in writing and discussing poetic assignments, and each teacher can make appropriate arrangements to insure that such activity is an element of a student's final evaluation for the course. But teachers should not assign a letter or numerical grade to each separate piece of poetic writing. In non-English classes poetic writing serves primarily as a learning tool rather than as an evaluation instrument. Consciously and frequently using poetic language will not make us all Shakespeares, but it will give us better opportunities for uniting theory and practice, reason and imagination, knowledge and action.

Epilogue: A Parable with Responses

A Parable

There once was a dog who barked bountifully. He barked to say hello, to silence the darkness, to express hunger, gossip with neighbors, to frighten intruders, and just to hear his own voice. His Family of Masters trained him to curtail his barking, and this made the house comfortable and peaceful. The dog was permitted to bark to say hello, to express hunger, and to frighten intruders; but never was he allowed to bark to silence the darkness, gossip with neighbors, or hear his own voice. He was fed and kept warm in. exchange for obedience. Then one day many years later a rat came to the cradle in the darkness. The dog wanted to bark at the intruder, but fearing to bark in the night, the dog listened to the sounds of the feast, detached and transcendent.

The Obedient Dog
(Student Response)

This is quite an odd piece of writing. The tone of it is one of "matter of fact" and sort of unemotional. The dog is happy and free to express himself until his masters get tired of his forms of expression. They only want him as a functional dog to bark hello, to express hunger, and to frighten intruders. In a way, the dog was "threatened" not to do anything but function because he was fed and kept warm in exchange for obedience. Then when the intruder came in the darkness, the dog, being obedient, kept silent as the rat feasted.

The way the grotesque last scene is calmly and quietly portrayed catches the reader's attention to the fact that an injustice has been committed.

The first "interpretation" that came to my mind was that the creative abilities of an "abnormal" person was stifled to fit them into the mold of society. When the time came that these creative abilities would be very useful, the person had become so conditioned to not using his abilities, that he just calmly sat back and watched the situation.

The Dog Barking
(Student Response)

Oh come on! Let's not be ridiculous! Think for a second what a dog's bark sounds like—think over, and over and over. It tends to get on the average person's nerves. Now one first reads this story he is filled with emotions. Oh that poor little doggie so inhibited—so suppressed—and the "feast in the cradle"—what a tear jerking device! This sounds like something written by a bleeding heart liberal!

This was first of all a very stupid dog to have around—he can't tell the difference between the rat and the darkness—has this dog no common sense?—It should—the author of this rubbish has given it every other human characteristic possible!

I especially like the line "He is fed and kept warm in exchange for his obedience." The author makes it sound like if the dog had only been forced to shut up with the threat of the very denial of his food and health! Listen if he wants to live there, he like everyone else in this world, better learn that there are concessions to make—rules to follow—and above all try and be considerate of others. Also the author tries to smooth over the fact that he could bark at all to say hello, express hunger, and TO FRIGHTEN INTRUDERS. What was the rat? A house guest? If I were they I'd put the worthless beast to sleep!

What poetic language does—both in the reading and the writing—is provide us with a unique perspective on experience, valuable because it allows us to place our personal interpretation in a social and cultural context, and because it allows the dominant social and cultural interpretation to be subject to personal understanding. Thus the process by which individuals and communities become interdependent is active and informed and not passive and by default. Such is the purpose and the power of the poetic function of language.

Notes

1. *Science and Human Values* (New York: Harper and Row, 1972), p. 8.

2. Nancy Martin, P. D'Arcy, B. Newton, and R. Parker, *Writing and Learning across the Curriculum 11–16* (London: Ward Lock Educational, 1976), p. 86.

3. "Language and Learning across the Curriculum," *Fforum* 2, no. 2 (1981): 94.

4. James Britton, Tony Burgess, Nancy Martin, Alex McLeod, and Harold Rosen, *The Development of Writing Abilities (11–18)* (London: Macmillan

Education, 1975). My discussion of the functions of written language is based on this book. See particularly pages 74–87.

5. *The Composing Processes of Twelfth Graders* (Urbana, Ill.: NCTE, 1971), p. 89.

6. Participant and spectator are Britton's terms; for further explanation of these concepts see Britton, pp. 79–83.

7. Herbert J. Muller, "A Note on Methods of Analysis," in *The Limits of Language,* ed. Walker Gibson (New York: Hill and Wang, 1962), pp. 30–31.

8. Albert Einstein and Leopold Infeld, *The Evolution of Physics* (New York: Simon and Schuster, 1938), p. 33.

9. My thanks to William Sewell of Michigan Technological University for permission to describe this exercise and quote the informal paper he wrote.

10. Britton, pp. 81–83.

7 Shaping Experience: Narration and Understanding

James Kalmbach
Michigan Technological University

William Powers
Michigan Technological University

In his account of a brief captivity by Indians, the famous Pocahontas account, John Smith tells of a ceremony in which Indian dancers and singers told of their own knowledge, their country, and the sea and into that narrative fitted some of what they had learned of Smith's own country. They carried the ceremony out for three days. Smith wrote, "The meaning whereof they told him was to know if he intended them well or no." The Indians attempted to understand John Smith by telling a story about him.

For the purposes of writing across the curriculum, one of the most significant aspects of narration is the convincing way it discloses that certain events taken together can make up a singular experience. The Indians who captured John Smith tried to combine their experiences with his into a story. Narrative is unique in its capacity to give a form or shape to the otherwise unlinked chain of experience.

Consider two texts:

> stars faded
> eastern sky grew light
> clouds above horizon turned pink
> sun rose

> I woke early, restless and still tired at first. Lying in bed, I saw the stars fade and the eastern sky grow light; then the clouds above the horizon turned pink, and watching the sun rise, I was glad I was awake and starting a new day.

The differences between the list and the paragraph are conspicuous: (1) The list is a passively reported register of events; the paragraph is a narration of those same events as they were experienced by someone. (2) The list does not develop into a unified text except insofar as a reader may recognize a chronological sequence in it; the narrative does develop—it builds to a conclusion in which the narrator relates the import of the sunrise. Although both the list and the narrative are chronological reports, the list is simply a chronicle; the narrative is a recounting of a personal experience, an experience told as a perception of events which forms a single coherent whole.

Here is another narrative:

> Three years ago I moved into one of the old houses near the Michigan Tech campus with six other men. Several of the other men had high quality stereos. We soon found that slamming doors or walking briskly across the floor would cause the house to shake; this in turn caused tone arms to skip across albums being played. This annoyed the stereo owners and listeners greatly; it caused poor sound and damaged the stereo equipment.
>
> For my ME370 (Analysis of Dynamic Systems) class project I chose to do an engineering analysis of this problem and tried to develop a viable solution to it. The analysis consisted of the writing of a computer program, and lab work to verify the program results.
>
> The solution developed centers on the use of a foam rubber material which is used to help dampen the vibrations in the turntable's environment before they reach the turntable.

This narrative is a little different from the narrative paragraph above. It also tells of a significant experience, but it is intended to introduce a technical report, rather than to relate a personal experience. The first narrative ends with a personal conclusion, "I was glad I was awake and starting a new day." It is introspective. The second narrative ends with a solution to the tone arm skip. It is not introspective. Both narratives depend on the experience and perception of the narrator. In the first the narrator seems to address only herself. In the second, the narrator is reaching out to a different reader, a reader to whom he wishes to introduce a problem that needs solving.

To generalize from these examples, two characteristics of narrative that relate to classroom writing are:

1. Narrative is one way students can articulate for themselves what they know or can become comfortable with what they have found out. It can be a part of the process of learning.

2. Narrative is also a way students may approach an audience or come to terms with some of the special qualities of a particular audience.

Narrative and Learning

A narrative never exhaustively represents a series of real life events since the multitude of details, sensations, impressions, and segmentations simultaneous with any experience are limitless. Narrators must sort out from such quantity of detail only those events which seem important or significant to the story at hand. Telling a story necessarily involves a process of *selection*. In the engineer's narrative, there are few details about the three years of living that the story covers. Only those events which affected the tone arms—slamming doors and brisk walking—are reported.

This process of selection is a form of understanding. A narrative conveys an understanding of events, not the events themselves. Narrating helps the narrator come to grips with an experience and comprehend it, at least somewhat. To ask students to write a narrative about an experiment, a project, or even what happened in class one day is to invite them to create an understanding of these experiences.

One fairly simple way to demonstrate how understanding is formed through narrative is to ask for two short narratives on the same topic. After the first narrative has been written, make available some information which will change what the student knows about that topic. The second narrative should reflect the changed understanding. When the narratives are compared the growth or change in the student's knowledge about the topic will be apparent.

This exercise works well when the topic is one with which the class has some familiarity—perhaps through a prerequisite course in chemistry, physics, math, or history—and the students write first about their previous encounter with the topic. After new aspects of the topic are presented, the students can be asked to write a narrative of their second encounter. Here are two narratives written a week apart by John R., a student in a class in physics for nonscience students:

> January 16.
> When was the last time I read about Mendel? It was in a sex education class in junior high school—that's where. It was so-o-o bad. But I still remember something about pink and white sweet-peas and about numbers, maybe because that was what that course was like. It was sex education and we spent the whole time on anatomy and numbers. Mendel is just one more set of dead or displaced numbers.

> January 23.
> When Mr. Porridge said to write about Mendel, I said more dead or displaced numbers. I wrote that down. What I have found out since then is that Poisson predicted the number of soldiers who would be kicked to death by horses in any given year in the German cavalry, that there are about seventy-five people bitten by dogs every year in New York City, and that the odds in roulette depend on zero coming up once in thirty-seven times. Mendel in sex education was pretty dull, but fitted into figures about probability, he goes better. And there is something to puzzle over, as Mr. Porridge says.

What kind of understanding has taken place in the interval between these two narratives? John shows that he understands something about contextual perception. Mendel in the context of a dull class in sex education seemed to be dull and displaced. Mendel in the context of probability theory, which John found appealing, became an interesting sort of statistician.

This pair of narratives shows what John understood, something of the nature of contextual perception, and what John did *not* know, or could not bring to bear, specific statements revealing his understanding of the associations in probability between Mendel and Poisson. In this case, the narratives provided his teacher with a particular follow-up assignment—the teacher had John write a one page definition of probability theory illustrated with reference to Mendel and to Poisson.

Another way teachers can get narratives from students about class experience is to assign a narrative log, a notebook in which a narrative is written about what is done for each new assignment or project. The log then becomes a record of the students' understanding of the class, and as such it may be useful to teachers as well as students. Here is an example. A teacher had given a class an assignment which required each student to use a microcomputer. For students unfamiliar with the machine, the teacher had written a set of directions. As a part of the assignment, the students were also asked to write about their first experience with the microcomputer. The teacher thought that writing about the machine would help the students to understand it and also show how effective the directions were. Here is Sue B.'s narrative of her experience:

> When I went in, no one was around, so I found my disk and figured out how to sign it out and how to put it in. But then, I couldn't follow what to expect from the manual when it said hit "execute" and hit "insert" and the underlining part just kind of blew me away. I didn't even try it out. I got a few things on it and then it took me awhile to figure out how to get the machine to accept my information for good. I didn't run any printout the first time I was on it. I spent about two hours just trying to figure it out. And I just felt like dropping the class. This sudden fear that it is never going to work out. But since then I've used it a couple of times and it's really easy now.

Writing such a narrative can contribute to learning to use a microcomputer and to becoming comfortable and confident with it. In her narrative, Sue moves quickly from a moment of desperation, "this sudden fear that it is never going to work out" to the realization that she has in fact become competent and comfortable with a microcomputer. Her understanding of the experience changes, in part, because of the act of writing about it. The narrative also showed something about the teacher's part in the effort. Despite Sue's initial difficulties, the manual the teacher had written was adequate. Narrative logs of their work through the term can provide students with a record of their success in the course; they can also give teachers a running assessment of class assignments.

Narration and the Audience

The narratives we have considered so far have mainly been useful to the writers themselves. But narrative is also commonly written because it is useful to a broader audience. The narrative about tone arm skip examined earlier was in fact an introductory narrative for a five page report. It presented a personal experience, troubles with stereo tone arms skipping, as the basis for the problem addressed by the technical report. The narrative would be useful to all readers of the report. Contrast it with the narrative which follows, this one a progress report assigned as one stage in the composing of a longer report.

Progress Report on Tropical Fish Disease Manual

Project Description

The subject of my article is tropical fish diseases. While examining some of the common infections, it will point out symptoms and treatments also. To prevent reinfection, a chapter will be devoted on disease prevention. The finished product will be a reference manual in which alphabetically-indexed disease symptoms will refer to the page with the disease's description and treatment. For further information, please refer to my proposal submitted on October 21, 1980.

Work Completed

My work done on this article has progressed to the point of locating multiple sources from which I will do research. My preliminary work includes research and notetaking from these sources and basic organization of diseases with symptoms and treatments. See attachments from proposal letter dated October 21, 1980.

Work Schedule

As indicated by the work done, I have a considerable amount of work to do. By next weekend, November 8, 1980, I should have all the information that I need to begin the final organization. I realize that I am pushed for time, but I assure you that I will complete the project by November 14, 1980.

Written for the teacher, this progress report explains what has been done on the project so far, something both the student and the teacher need to understand. The narrative confirms a double commitment: by the student to join in a classroom process of developing a specific paper for a specific time and place, and also by the teacher to take a formal part in this process as a guide along the way and as an arbiter of the final work.

This narrative might, however, have been assigned in a different way for a different audience, perhaps at different stages in the project. For example, it might have been assigned as a narrative in the form of a letter to the class—not to the teacher—about the experience of doing the work. It might offer at least one piece of advice to other persons with projects to do. Such a letter can be used in any class in which reports are required. Later in his project, Richard B. wrote the following letter to his class:

> Dear Class:
>   When I was in junior high my parents bought an aquarium and put some goldfish in it. They wanted to get me interested in something to learn discipline and science or something like that.
>   That part went all right. I learned a lot about fish and in the last few years I have even made a little money selling some. I also lost a lot of fish, and learned something about fish diseases. So I thought I would write my manual about tropical fish diseases.
>   It was easy to get the information together for the report; most of it I knew and half the books I had. One good thing I did was to use index cards. I made a card for each disease. Then I wrote the symptoms of the disease on each card. But I stalled on the writing as long as I could. And I spent hours on a paragraph when I started.
>   Then I tried something from this class and got the draft done. I did the nonstop writing we do in class. I thought that to get a five-page fish report, if I could do ten pages nonstop I might have something. So I wrote ten pages without stopping. One page had nothing on it but the word fish about two hunded times. Then I went back and did the last line from the previous page over again and got going. In about forty-five minutes I had about ten pages.
>   That's it. I cut that down and worked in the notes, but the five pages I turned in as my draft were five pages straight out of my nonstop.
>   My advice is, try it.
>
>   Richard B.

Richard's letter begins with his experiences raising tropical fish. This beginning helps readers understand why he wanted to write his manual just as the narrative about tone arm skip helped readers understand the problem that technical report attempted to solve. The subject matter of Richard's letter, however, is not tropical fish but the common experience of the class. What organizes the events of the narrative is an understanding of this experience. His narrative will help some students who are having similar problems writing their manuals and it will reinforce the experience of others.

But the subject of the letter is not simply writing—it is also the techniques which the class had been practicing. The letter describes the specific usefulness of notecards in this assignment. In a more abstract way it helps to explain the usefulness of classification in thought and analysis, since the system of cards which Richard employed was also a system of classification.

Richard had been simply directed to give advice to the class. But in giving that advice, he sorted out what was useful to him from the common experience of the class and thus provided a kind of narrative scrutiny of a portion of the course. Such scrutiny should be useful across the curriculum.

Here are some further kinds of narrative assignments:

> Ask students to look over their notes from a selected period of time and to write a narrative comment, something like: "When I look back over yesterday's notes (or last week's), the first thing that strikes me is . . ." It sometimes works to ask for two paragraphs, one begining with this sentence, the second beginning, "The next thing I see or think of is . . ." This assignment can be written for the class as an audience as well as for the teacher. It may provide the basis for a class discussion of a particular problem or be a good assignment for a teacher to carry out when preparing an exam, as a means of learning how well a class is prepared and how subtle or demanding an exam they will learn from.

> Ask students to role play. Ask them to tell about what they are doing in a class as if they were persons outside the classroom. Instead of a book report, someone in an English class can write an opinion of a book as a member of a school board who has been asked to review some things used in the school. Instead of a lab report, someone in a science course may be asked to write a summary of a lab experiment as viewed by a visitor to the school from another time or another place—and classmates may then be asked to evaluate the report simply on the basis of their ability to recognize the experiment and to replicate it.

> Ask students to write narrative introductions to even the most technical of their reports; teachers may find those introductions useful in identifying the strengths and weaknesses of those reports.

Teachers can write narratives of their own to the class, possibly in the form of letters. Instead of relying on the ability of a class to take notes, teachers can give them a letter on occasion which addresses some current topic and which can provide a basis for classroom discussion or for other further learning.

Narrative writing is valuable in any course which requires papers, projects, reports, or readings. Communicating experience is a fundamental function of language. Transforming experience into words requires both an understanding of the experience and an awareness of audience demands and interests. Narrative forms include: letters, informal classroom writing, notebook writing, progress reports, and formal introductions to technical reports; all can be used in the classroom as a means of helping students find out what they are learning, as a means of helping teachers assess the progress of learning, and as a means for both students and teachers to respond to particular audiences.

8 In Search of Meaning: Readers and Expressive Language

Bruce Petersen
Michigan Technological University

When people read they are searching for meaning. They generate ideas in response to books—ideas which depend on our experiences, expectations, and prior knowledge about the text and its subject. Put another way: people generalize from the information they get when they read books. One frustration we face as teachers is that students' generalizations are often quite different from either our own or from the generalizations of other students. Apart from those students who simply do not read the assignment we all have known students who honestly try to understand reading assignments but whose responses orally or in exams often seem idiosyncratic at best.

In a literature class, I try to be open-minded and allow for wide leeway in "interpretation" because I know that people come to fiction or poetry with different personalities and different backgrounds. I would be less likely to accept variants in the science or mathematics class—after all, here we are not supposed to be dealing with interpretation, but with fact. However, we learn largely by using language—by talking, listening, writing, and reading, and these language activities are uniquely interrelated in each individual, and socially interconnected among individuals through linguistic conventions and agreements. In other words, what we learn and what we know depends on the use and manipulation of both the private and public worlds of our language system.

Work in cognitive psychology suggests that learning proceeds in stages. We learn new concepts by assimilating them into what we already know. The first stage in learning a new concept is analogous to a "private" dialogue. We proceed as if we were talking to ourselves—attempting to fit new and unfamiliar information into the world view we already possess. For example, reading research demonstrates that students comprehend written material best when they explicitly make hypotheses in their own language about what they read in books. They then confirm or refute these hypotheses by reviewing or discussing the text individually or in groups. Personal prediction and communal confirmation are at the heart of the learning process. One way to see this is to examine the way people read a technical text. Readers, like writers, proceed from a personal matrix of experiences, facts, social conventions, and conceptual and moral development towards creating meaning from a text. Kenneth Goodman puts it this way: "What message the reader produces is partly dependent on what the writer intended, but also *very much dependent on what the reader brings to the particular text.*"[1] Whenever we use language as a learning tool we follow thinking processes which are mirrored in the processes of writing and reading.

An Experiment in the Reading Process

It is now standard practice to conceive of learning in "scientific" or "technical" subjects as different in nature from learning in the "humanities." We can see this difference in the common conception of the way we read and process "transactional" or technical writing compared to the way we process aesthetic or poetic writing. Anne Eisenberg's definition of scientific writing, from her text, *Reading Technical Books,* may be taken as representative: "language in science is special and particular. Each term has a very precise meaning. This is entirely different from the way language is used in everyday life."[2] That is, language in the sciences is referential (transactional) and meaning resides simply in a correct response by the reader to the text, while in everyday life, or in expressive and poetic writing, readers constantly make new meanings out of a conversation or a text based on personal associations.

I hope to show, first, that this concept of the processes involved in both "transactional" writing and "transactional" reading is too narrow; and second, that because of this fact, pedagogy in the sciences would benefit from using students' written responses to both texts and research data. This is demonstrated, in part, by the fact that readers of scientific prose in textbooks, scientific journals, or science magazines for popular consumption respond in ways remarkably similar to the ways readers respond to aesthetic works (poetry, in particular). Readers learn by transforming their own personal associative responses to a text into an objective form which they consider knowledge.

The following experiment in reader response helps to demonstrate these ideas. I asked a number of faculty members to respond to a three-paragraph section from an article in *Scientific American*. Each reader was instructed to write "what the passage means to you." The sample follows:

Among the innovations that were once heavily supported and publicized but that have since fallen by the wayside one may remember fish-protein concentrates for human consumption and protein from single-cell algae grown on petroleum substrates. The proposals themselves are technically feasible, but they proved not to be economically viable and also resulted in food products people did not like. Opaque-2 maize (which has a high content of the essential amino acids lysine and tryptophan), antarctic krill and the wheat-rye hybrid triticale all seem to hold promise, but it is too early to predict their success. In short, it would be unwise to bank on technological breakthrough for the long-term solution to food shortages.

In retrospect one characteristic common to unsuccessful food innovations is that they were supported "from above" and had little relevance to the problems perceived by the people the innovations were supposed to help. A successful new technology has to fit the entire socioeconomic system in which it is to find a place. Security of crop yield, palatibility and costs are much more significant than the advocates of new technologies have recognized. For example, the better protein quality in tortillas made from opaque-2 maize is only a second order benefit to a poor family on the margin of subsistence if the new maize does not match the yields of older varieties or is more vulnerable to insects. There is optimism that new high-yielding varieties of opaque-2, with harder kernals to thwart insects, will be more widely accepted.

To such technical difficulties must be added a second set of complications: economic and political power relations strongly influence the outcome of those innovations that are put to use. In the Anglo-American tradition Schultz and most other economists stress private profitability as the key factor in guiding technical change. Actually profitability is neither a necessary nor a sufficient condition for a new technology to be adopted, let alone for it to benefit the poor.[3]

Readers' Responses

Now, consider the ways in which readers responded to the passage in terms of (1) the literal meanings they derived, (2) the various levels of abstraction in which they wrote their responses, and (3) the stylistic choices they made as they wrote. The readers in this case were faculty members in the Department of Humanities at Michigan Technological University.[4]

Ann: The passage says . . . it would be unwise to bank on technological breakthrough for the long-term solution to food shortages because implementation of technological innovations is affected by the context within which they are to be implemented. Factors which complicate implementation include technical ones (security of crop yield, palatability, and costs) as well as economic and political ones.

Bob· Thesis: Uses of new technology in increasing food supplies have been frustrated by inadequate research, socioeconomic problems, and political difficulties.

Chris: Innovative food products, designed to reduce food shortages, have not been as successful as was hoped . . . though many . . . were technically feasible. . . . If we can learn to look at the entire socioeconomic picture we may yet find some success.

David: The writer argues that technological advances are not in themselves sufficient to insure the acceptance of new products. Examples . . . illustrate failure . . . due to . . . such factors as consumer tastes and perceptions, environmental constraints, and the socioeconomic power relationships in the marketplace.

Ellen: The author argues against the feasibility of purely technological solutions to food shortages and malnutrition.

Fred: The passage shows the failure of pure technology to solve the crisis of food production and protein production in the underdeveloped world. The passage means that technology must be tempered and/or supplemented by sociological and ecological concerns. . . . But who didn't know this that paid any attention to what was and is going on in the world. Political power doesn't shift when we have as a central interest avoiding "instability."

Glen: . . . technocrats tend to look at things from their own point of view [not from the view] of the people they are trying to help . . . [the passage is] an exercise in the nature of reading and says to me something about confidence in reading. The author throws around a lot of big words in the beginning, trying to convince you that you know nothing about what is to follow.

Harold: The writer is aware of the danger of applying technology blindly, without taking into account social or environmental conditions that may affect the success or failure of the new technology. The voice of the speaker . . . is muted by his/her easy adaptation of clichés—"technically feasible," "fallen by the wayside," "economically viable," etc. . . . I hear old voices from 1968 being resurrected—good voices—[but] I guess I'm a little tired of the message—I feel a sense of futility and frustration. I don't know what to make of the information.

Ingrid:
If you ain't got the do-re-me, boys
If you ain't got the do-re-me
All the techno-inno won't do you no good
If you ain't got the do-re-me.

A Discussion of Readers' Responses

A single reading of these responses might suggest general agreement about one point: technological solution to the food shortage in under-developed countries has not succeeded as well as anticipated. However, I can say this only as a guess about the possible communal agreement which might be achieved by these readers. Clearly, they believe the passage says something about food and technology in the Third World —but even on this fundamental level there are a variety of readings. Their responses to the paragraphs show marked stylistic, syntactic, and semantic differences, which imply that readers of transactional texts affect the meaning of the text just as they would in response to other types of text. Readers will arrive at some core of agreed meaning—but they also show marked differences in word choice, in inference, in complexity of thought, and in personal involvement. In short, the readers have learned different things from the reading and have responded out of their private language systems. As will be shown, these can only be developed into shared meaning through group discussion. Without discussion of the responses readers will move farther apart as their original perspectives and hypotheses shape the meaning they would find in any extension of the text.

Ann quotes directly that it "would be unwise to bank on techno-logical breakthrough." It may well be that the text says this, although the second paragraph also seems to imply that we may expect useful development. Bob argues that the uses of technology "have been frus-trated" by various factors. I believe personal interests and experiences shaped these two opposing sentiments. Ann seems to feel that meaning here resides in as strict reliance on denotation as possible—the less paraphrase, the better. Bob, on the contrary, attempts a succinct para-phrase which leaves out detail that Ann includes. However, if word count alone is considered, Bob's and Ann's responses show only mini-mal differences. Further reflection on the text in isolation will not provide a resolution to these differences since both responses seem justified (and their authors might well go to some length to demon-strate why).

Chris, David, and Ellen see less technological failure than Ann and Bob. Chris says that innovative food products "have not been as suc-cessful as was hoped"; David says that such technologies "are not in themselves sufficient"; and Ellen says that solutions cannot be "purely" technological (but they can be partially so—a considerable contrast to Ann).

Even considering these differences, which are considerable and not trivial in terms of their implications for cost, political concerns, and priorities for future development, the authors of these responses show a marked attempt to stick to denotative meaning. That is, the authors attempt to say what they "took away" from the reading and do not refer explicitly to what they brought to it. In a classroom, objective agreement will result only when students examine the reasons for these differences, reasons which I suspect reflect subjective responses of the authors to technology, to the style of the article (and their decision to mimic it), and to the issue of political problems in the Third World. These readers need to see how their view of language shapes the meaning they derive from the response. Does Bob, for example, think the nontechnological bias of native populaces influences what might otherwise be successful technology? Does David see hope in a proper combination of technology, ethnology, and politics? These questions shape the individual meaning each author derives from the text because they reflect unspoken experiences and affects. I, for example, would be interested in Ann's thoughts on computers.

Fred, Glen, Harold, and Ingrid move toward quite different reactions both to the text itself and to their understanding of the word *meaning* given in the instructions. Clearly, for these respondents the word suggests speculation, generalization, and inference. Their responses are both more obviously (that is, on the surface) personal and extend into areas of thought related only by the reader's associations. Fred comments on his frustration that this knowledge about technological limitations hasn't brought about change of some sort already. Indeed, the "frustration" which Bob mentioned is quite at odds with the "frustration" Fred and Harold feel. Perhaps, in discussion, Chris would join in making explicit his frustration that success was not what was hoped.

Glen sees the paragraphs separated from this context and as part of a larger concept—of the inevitable inertia to be overcome in all large scale change. Comments on style were offered verbally by a number of readers but they edited these comments out. They felt meaning and style had no interrelation—a concept which would need considerable discussion in light of the variety of styles these responses show. Indeed, I believe that Ingrid's response, in particular, is a conscious and aggressive attack on the style of the article. Of course, I cannot "know" this until I discuss the matter with the author.

Implications for Pedagogy

Apart from the interest of stylistic differences I consider two points about the responses significant: (1) their base in personal associations and language discussed above, and (2) their various levels of abstraction. Ann, Bob, Chris, Glen, and Ellen report on or summarize the material. Harold offers a generalization and narration of his experience while he read. Fred, Glen, and Ingrid, however, make generalizations and speculations about meanings inferred from the passage. These several levels of abstraction show great similarities to James Moffett's "levels of discourse."[5] At the same time the apparent expressive base of the writing mirrors James Britton's argument that the decision to write, to make meaning, to decide on significance is grounded in the experience of the writer. There is growing evidence which suggests that this expressive base of learning extends to readers and researchers. What are the pedagogical implications of the foregoing discussion? First, that a test or examination given to students who have not shared their responses to common reading may not test any individual student's ability to develop knowledge from a given textbook. Indeed, by examining students' responses we can demonstrate that the student will have developed knowledge—the problem is that even with technical and scientific reading it may not be the knowledge we expect. Our test then doesn't examine the student's knowledge; it doesn't tell us how intelligent this student is, nor does it show us whether or not this student has read the material. The test may tell us only that the student doesn't know what we know.

What techniques can we use to develop a body of knowledge understood in common by members of our classes? One successful method used in literature classes depends on making connections among the thinking processes involved in writing and reading and on the need for students to make explicit both their predictions and confirmations about their reading. Reading any text is, as we have seen, a matter of predicting, confirming, and composing meaning. But I believe that only when students weave their personal knowledge of texts and experience into a pattern through writing and discussion as a group can they say, "We know."

A Pedagogical Model

David Bleich, in his book *Subjective Criticism*, argues that knowledge about anything depends on language and its primary role in symbolizing experience.[6] Bleich considers it pedagogically imperative that students analyze both books and their written responses to the books. I have used Bleich's theory successfully in several literature classes by asking students to respond to novels first in writing. If you consider the following example from one of my classes, you can see that the student's response is expressive—Martha is working out her associations to a passage from D. H. Lawrence's novel, *Sons and Lovers*, in terms of her past personal experience:

The beginning of the passage evokes memories of the typical motherly response I was used to when growing up. There is instinctive psychology put to use when Mrs. Radford allows Paul to make his own choice about whether or not to go to bed, but (she points out), it is late. . . . "Do what you want, but don't forget what I believe is right." . . . It is a soft weapon.

It reminds me of a summer evening at the dinner table when I was told that I must eat a carrot . . . I thought they were vile tasting things and that I was being tortured. . . . As the family left the table one by one to go out in the back yard there was finally myself and my mother who firmly coaxed me to eat my carrot. She finally left for the yard, as I gazed with disappointment at that object of distaste. She thought she could get me to finish it off, just as Mrs. Radford really believed that Paul was going to bed to sleep, but of course I took my golden opportunity and promptly disposed of the carrot. Dear Mom thought I had eaten it.

I also related to Paul's apology for his cold fingers which also bothered me the first time I danced with some boys in a ballroom dancing class in junior high. Would some boy drop my fingers as he would ice cubes?

One of the most important aspects of sharing these types of responses in class is the student's recognition of the varied sources of their associations. As lecturers, teachers all too often assume that their emotional responses and their students' develop in wholly analogous ways. On the contrary, although the feelings evoked may be common to both student and teacher those feelings usually emerged from a variety of sources. For the student above it is important to see that her reaction to being forced by her mother to eat a carrot was similar to Paul and Clara's reaction to Mrs. Radford's machinations; but it is more important for her to see the variety of events which sparked similar feelings in her peers, for by doing that she and her classmates create a meaning in common for the experiences of the reading which did not exist before their discussion.

I ask students to consciously use their immediate responses to their readings to help them create knowledge about the text. I find that a fruitful study of literature arises from the students' personal working out of meaning through his or her responses followed by group discussion during which the class lists and compares their responses. In this way we collectively make or compose meanings as a group. Students do not feel that meaning is something they must discover in the words of the text. Rather, they begin to see that interpretation is primarily a communal activity. Bleich points out that this communal or collaborative act "is validated by the ordinary fact that when each person says what he sees, each statement will be substantially different. The response must therefore be the starting point for the study of aesthetic experience."[7]

The experiment in reader response which began this chapter suggests that the responses of students also should be a focus for study in scientific fields as well. The variety of responses to an "objective" group of paragraphs shows that students need to think about why they responded as they did—not that they responded "incorrectly." Of course, the responses are useful to the teacher as well. By examining the style and order of ideas in the responses, the teacher can tell which students' language is closest in structure to that of the passage. There are trivial and inappropriate responses—there are responses which show clear problems of comprehension or difficulty in identifying significant information. The teacher also can identify those students whose style of response is so different from the original text that the response seems simply idiosyncratic—consider Ingrid's response to the piece from *Scientific American*. The way people derive meaning from a text is closely related to the way they structure the text in their own words. A response statement can also reveal similarities and differences between the structure of the student's language and the structure of the text.[8]

Responses may be obtained through several kinds of questions. One is simply to ask students for a paraphrase of a text. The response should be written without the text available. Or students may be asked to say what a chapter, or problem means. In this case the text should be made available since the student will often use interpretation to answer the question. Whatever method is used to generate responses the class must share them in groups. The students themselves will identify trivial responses (and the teacher can find ways to guide a discussion which seems to get off track). In classes which deal with formal symbolic systems—mathematics, for example—it is often useful to have students reformulate equations and concepts verbally. Teachers might use short (five minute) journal writes such as "Discuss the statement, 'Factoring and finding a product are reverse processes.'" A more complex question would also provide material for extended class discussion in an algebra class: "Think of an analogy in the nonmathematical world describing the relationship between a perfect square trinomial and its binomial square."[9]

Writing and Reading: The "Expressive" Connection

I have spoken already about connections among the various aspects of language use and their interconnections in learning. Reading, listening, speaking, and writing share an expressive or personal base which I believe constitutes the heart of the learning process in any discipline which depends on language or symbolic forms in its teaching and practice. James Britton in *The Development of Writing Abilities (11–18)* outlines a theory of writing development grounded on what he calls "expressive" writing.[10] Britton defines expressive writing as writing done for the self with the purpose of using language to follow "the unfolding of experiences and thoughts in the head, close to their emergence and close to the contours of thinking."[11] Writing, Britton argues, is grounded in the immediate, personal life of the writer. This does not mean, of course, that writing does not move into other less obviously personal modes; but it does mean that writing begins in the self and that the composing process is, in part, a search for appropriate modes of approach to an audience. The writer relates his work to his own experience; he must develop his thought on the basis of what he knows. "Whatever it is that provokes the decision to write . . . it soon comes to be seen in relation to all the writer's relevant previous experience. His conception, the way he explains to himself what he must do, is influenced by his involvement or lack of it."[12]

Because most writing implies, eventually, some audience, it is good practice for teachers to combine writing and speaking in the classroom: this provides an immediate audience. Talking about writing is valuable because talk is more expressive than writing and because, in Britton's words, "talk relies on an immediate link with listeners; . . . the rapid exchanges of conversation allow many things to go on at once —exploration, clarification, shared interpretation, insight into differences of opinion, illustration and anecdote, explanation of gesture, expression of doubt. . . ."[13] Britton's colleagues, in their research on writing across the curriculum extend this connection between writing and speech to encompass associations among writing, speech, listening, reading. "One of the major uses of language that concerns teachers is its use for learning: for trying to put new ideas into words, for testing out one's thinking on other people, for fitting together new ideas with old ones which will need to be done to bring about new understanding. These functions suggest active uses of language by the pupil, as opposed to passive reception. . . . 'Language' is the sum total of talking, listening, reading and writing. No one of these four modes is more important than the others, and all should be developed equally."[14]

Consider, in this context, the responses to the piece of writing on food production. If we remember that the respondents arrived at various interpretations of both the material and the instructions, we can see the immediate pedagogical value of analyzing the various responses in a group. Now the respondents can test their own hypotheses of the passage's meaning against both the text and against the collective experiences and hypotheses of other readers. The personal nature of the responses does not intrude on the development of learning; rather, it enhances it by showing the personal bases from which to begin learning. The teacher's role is to assist students in making logical connections, to keep students returning to the text to confirm their own hypothesis, and to help the students codify their developing knowledge. The teacher encourages the process of thought by progressing from expressive language in journals, diaries, first drafts, and response notebooks to discussion of that language and then to more formal uses such as essays, argumentation, research papers, and final drafts.

Expressive Language and Thinking Complexity

James Moffett's work in discourse theory suggests a similar need for teachers to follow a logical progression in language development based on cognitive theory.[15] Moffett argues that students learn best by moving in a logical and orderly progression through levels of abstraction (report, narration, generalization, and speculation) and levels of audience distance (reflection, conversation, correspondence, and publication). The ability to make higher level abstractions comes, Moffett argues, from "letting students try to symbolize raw phenomena of all kinds at all levels of abstraction. . . ."[16] Moffett's suggestions for a curriculum mean students must each struggle with data on a personal level; they do not "know" in any but a trivial way when they receive "knowledge" as empirical fact to be memorized from a teacher, and, more significantly, they do not develop an ability to make the abstractions which the teacher (or someone) had to make to decide on the importance of any discrete piece of data in the first place.

Consider again the responses to the *Scientific American* article. They are, as we have seen, expressive writing, but they are written on several different levels of abstraction. We need to remember that expressive writing does not represent simplistic thought. Indeed, the various levels of thought discussed by Moffett each may appear in expressive writing. An expressive response to language, to a laboratory experiment, or to raw data may describe, narrate, generalize, or speculate. The move toward transactional or poetic writing is not necessarily a movement into more complex or abstract thought patterns; it is primarily a movement toward a different audience.

Our language becomes less and less personal as we move outward from the expressive base—first we think to ourselves, then we speak to others whom we know about our ideas ("What do you think of this?"), then we may move toward an audience from whom we receive less immediate feedback (as we would write a letter to a friend, or editor), and finally we may produce a finished product on the assumption that we will get little or no feedback. Britton suggests that this process (perhaps internalized in experienced writers) occurs whenever we write. What is significant for my purpose here is that the process is the same for both literary and technical language.

This outline of an audience's distance from a writer deals only with the function which the writing serves and the relation between the reader and writer. Another aspect of language, perhaps even more important, concerns levels of thought complexity. Moffett classifies language use into four major categories of abstraction: Tautologic (or speculation); Analogic (or generalization); Narration; Report.[17]

It is important to remember that any of these levels of abstraction can apply to language used for either a poetic or transactional function; that is, we may communicate on any level of abstraction while our language serves any function. A poem, for example, may be written about as a report (paraphrase), as a narration of the reader's experience as he or she read the poem, as a generalization about the poem's connotative meanings, or as speculation about the relation of the meaning to events in the future. A diary may be as speculative as a formal scientific paper, a letter may narrate or generalize, and the proceedings of a professional organization may be reported on or described. By asking students to use expressive writing or to share their expressive responses to a mathematics text or problem, for example, we are not asking for less complex thought. On the contrary, we hope for a greater range of speculation because the student is not being graded or evaluated on a journal or rough draft. What we are asking for is the student's personal commitment to and responsibility for his evolving language system. The use of expressive writing or of reader responses is predicated on the common sense belief that language is the developmental, personal, and psychological foundation of learning in the individual. Research in both cognitive and psychoanalytic psychology appears to affirm this judgment.[18]

A Diagrammatic Model

I suggest that the reading process has direct connections to Britton's and Moffett's concepts of the process of writing. Figure 1 shows the theoretical matrix of expressive language and its relationship to both the function and uses of language. The diagram shows the relationships between expressive language—language close to our feelings, associations, and prior knowledge—and more formal uses of language, the transactional and poetic. The diagram also suggests that this matrix of personal language is central to learning because it forms the base for our thinking when we either produce or process language and thought. That is, we all begin thinking about new information through the resources of our past knowledge and associations. One of our jobs as teachers is to assist students in moving beyond personal knowledge to knowledge shared by a community, one shaped by cultural values and traditions. That is, we attempt to promote both individual learning and shared learning. Learning and the development of knowledge are, after all, social. Subjective thought, expressive language, becomes collective knowledge through communal agreement. Learning depends on shared knowledge.

But, it may be objected, science is a business of facts, mathematics a business of figures. Some people will argue that science is fundamentally different from literature. We have already examined one aspect of this argument when we studied the responses made to a "scientific" text. In addition, we may examine the definition of science offered by scientists themselves.

Physicist and mathematician, Jacob Bronowski shows that the same symbolic need which underlies all language underlies science; in fact, he claims science itself is a type of language—and it is a language which obeys a general law governing all language: ". . . consciousness depends wholly on our seeing the outside world in [terms of outside things]. And the problems of consciousness arise from putting reconstitution beside internalization, from our also being able to see ourselves as if we were objects in the outside world. That is the very nature of language; it is impossible to have a symbolic system without it."[19] Bronowski makes connections between poetry and science, and points

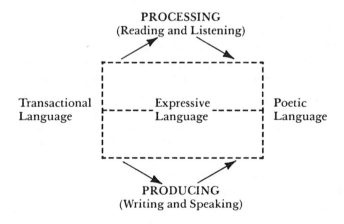

Figure 1.

out that what makes us human is our ability to work with symbolic images: the gift of imagination is not just a literary gift, "it is . . . characteristically human."[20] Bronowski shows that the "book of facts" image of science is wrong.

> [S]cience is not a collection of facts; it is the organization of the facts under general laws, and the laws in turn are held together by such concepts, such creations of the human mind, as gravitation. The facts are endless chaos . . . science is the human activity of finding an order in nature by organizing the scattered meaningless facts under universal concepts.[21]

If we think of Bronowski's statement in terms of Moffett's and Britton's concept of language and of the connections to learning we have now made among listening, writing, reading, speaking, then we see that our task as teachers is to assist the student in developing increased capacity to organize facts. We need to assist in the expansion of our students' ability to make abstractions and to express those abstractions.

But is this the common conception of learning in the sciences? Is it how students in our classes conceive of science as they sweat over the names of species and genus, the equations of inertia and rotational force, or the differential calculus? Students do need to know these things, but will they also learn the structure of their discipline, of its values beyond measurement and classification? More important in a practical sense is the question of whether more than a few students develop the abilities, founded in language, which Bronowski, for one, considers essential for scientists. That is, will students gain a passion for learning, the capacity for inference and speculation, an appreciation of originality, independence of thought, a regard for truth, tolerance of difference in opinion and thought, and an appreciation of dissent?[22] In order to accomplish these ends, we need to encourage students to examine the relationships between their own expressive words and the body of previously established knowledge in a discipline, that is, the connections between the student's language and the language of, for example, entymology, algebra, or physics.

It is not enough to ask questions which call for answers previously established; it is not enough to ask students to memorize algorithmic formulas. When teaching is carried on in this manner, students themselves do not learn to form the essential questions of their readings; they seldom respond to readings expressively; they do not easily use induction or speculation; nor do they often examine the growth and change taking place in their own language as a result of their experience with new bodies of knowledge.

I have suggested here one method which can assist students in the effort to relate their personal language to the language and structure of the books and writers they study. Using students' responses to their texts, encouraging students to share those responses, and analyzing the style and content of their responses will assist learners to integrate what they know with what they need to know. At the same time this method will develop new information, and new perspectives, on information we teach. Perhaps most significant, writing out and discussing responses will encourage students to examine the role that language plays in their learning in all courses.

Notes

1. P. David Allen and Dorothy J. Watson, eds., *Findings of Research in Miscue Analysis: Classroom Implications* (Urbana, Ill.: ERIC/NCTE, 1976), p. 58.

2. Anne Eisenberg, *Reading Technical Books* (Englewood Cliffs, N.J.: Prentice-Hall, 1978), p. 3.

3. Nevin S. Scrimshaw and Lance Taylor, "Food," *Scientific American* 243 (September 1980): 86–87.

4. The responses have been edited because of space limitations. Full text of responses may be obtained from Language Skills Laboratory, Department of Humanities, Michigan Technological University.

5. James Moffett, *Teaching the Universe of Discourse* (Boston: Houghton-Mifflin, 1968). Moffett describes four levels of discourse which he relates to cognitive levels: report, narration, analogic or generalization, and tautologic or speculation.

6. David Bleich, *Subjective Criticism* (Baltimore: The Johns Hopkins Press, 1978), pp. 38–67.

7. Bleich, p. 98.

8. For an introduction to top-level structure in reading see: Bonnie J. F. Meyer, David M. Brandt, and George J. Bluth, "Use of Top-level Structure in Text: Key for Reading Comprehension of Ninth-grade Students," *Reading Research Quarterly* 16, no. 1 (1980): 72–103.

9. I am indebted for these questions to Cynthia Nahrgang. She has developed techniques for using writing to teach mathematics in two courses in Algebra and Trigonometry at Michigan Technological University. Descriptions of the courses will be made available upon request.

10. James Britton, Tony Burgess, Nancy Martin, Alex McLeod, and Harold Rosen, *The Development of Writing Abilities (11–18)* (London: Macmillan Education, 1975). See, in addition, Randall Freisinger's article in the present volume.

11. Britton, p. 144. In the context of this paper consider also Britton's further comment: "Behind expressive writing lie the resources of speech and the ongoing accomplishment of spontaneous talk, which occupies much of the

lives of most of us and arguably informs more centrally than any other use of language our pupil's encounters with, and versions of, experience. . . . Expressive writing may operate as the matrix from which differentiated forms of mature writing are developed."

12. Britton, p. 23.

13. Britton, p. 29.

14. Mike Torbe, *Language across the Curriculum Guidelines for Schools* (1976; reprint ed., London: Ward Bond Educational, 1979), p. 7.

15. Moffett, *Teaching the Universe of Discourse.*

16. Moffett, p. 9.

17. Moffett, passim.

18. See, in particular: David Bleich, "The Motivational Character of Language and Symbol Formation," and "Epistemological Assumptions in the Study of Response," in *Subjective Criticism*, pp. 38-67, 97-133; John B. Carroll, "Words, Meaning, and Concepts," *Harvard Educational Review* 34 (Spring 1964): 178-202; Nan Elsasser and Vera P. John-Steiner, "An Interactionalist Approach to Advancing Literacy," *Harvard Educational Review* 47 (August 1977): 355-369; Paulo Freire, "The Adult Literacy Process as Cultural Action for Freedom," *Harvard Educational Review* 40 (May 1970): 205-225; Jurgen Habermas, *Knowledge and Human Interests*, tr. Jeremy J. Shapiro (1965; rpt. Boston: Beacon Press, 1972); Pinchas Noy, "The Psychoanalytic Theory of Cognitive Development," *The Psychoanalytic Study of the Child*, vol. 34 (New Haven: Yale University Press, 1979): 169-216; William Labov, *Language in the Inner-City: Studies in the Black English Vernacular* (Philadelphia: University of Pennsylvania Press, 1972); Jean Piaget, *Knowledge and Epistemology: Towards a Theory of Knowledge*, tr. Arnold Rosin (New York: Viking Press, 1971); *The Child and Reality: Problems of Genetic Psychology*, tr. Arnold Rosin (1972; reprint ed., Harmondsworth, England: Penguin, 1976); and Roger Poole, *Towards Deep Subjectivity* (New York: Harper and Row, 1972).

19. Jacob Bronowski, *The Origins of Knowledge and Imagination* (New Haven: Yale University Press, 1977), p. 38.

20. Jacob Bronowski, *A Sense of the Future* (Cambridge, Mass.: The MIT Press, 1977), p. 25.

21. Bronowski, *A Sense of the Future*, p. 255.

22. Bronowski, *A Sense of the Future*, pp. 214-220.

9 What Every Educator Should Know about Reading Research

Anne Falke
Michigan Technological University

The ability to read well is no longer something which college instructors take for granted in their students.[1] Most of us have noticed that the textbooks we use seem to get easier every year, but our students seem to have more and more trouble reading them.[2] Since reading is comprehension, students who cannot acceptably reconstruct the author's main idea, supporting ideas, and supporting facts, as well as make some critical evaluation of these things, cannot read for the purposes of the course, regardless of what types of material they read outside of class.

Many reasons exist for the inability to read a particular item. Sometimes the reader lacks sufficient background to properly interpret a particular item. Sometimes the information required for a particular reader to comprehend is missing. Sometimes a reader lacks the strategies necessary to read even the most elementary material acceptably. But for whatever causes, reading failure—the lack of understanding or misunderstanding of the author's literal or implied message—is a source of continual dismay for both student and instructor. Since reading is intimately entwined with the content of each academic class, all instructors must be concerned with the reading abilities of their students. Yet many instructors feel unsure of their abilities to teach reading in their classrooms. The purpose of this chapter is to acquaint teachers with the fundamentals of reading research in order that they may more confidently and effectively guide their students' learning.

What Reading Is and Is Not

Reading is the understanding of a message which has been encoded in a graphic display; in English the graphic display is printing or writing. Although reading is often defined as the decoding of letters into sound, it is not. A reader may, for example, know the sound-to-letter relationships in Spanish and be able to orally reproduce a

Spanish paragraph perfectly, but be unable to explain what the paragraph means. Often an inverse relationship exists between comprehension and perfect oral reading. Evidence indicates that in some cases comprehension actually precedes decoding. Many people, for instance, recognize the meaning of words long before they attempt to decode the letters into sound—that is, pronounce them.[3]

The information readers bring to what they read must therefore play an important part in how well they understand what they read. The "behind-the-eye" information may contribute as much as three-quarters of the information necessary to understand a passage.[4] If, for example, I wrote the sentence, "It is unlucky to have a black _____ cross your path," most people would not need to see the letters C-A-T to know that *cat* is the missing word. If, however, I wrote the sentence, "Michigan Technological University's best athletic team is its _____ team," most MTU students would not need the missing word to understand the meaning of the sentence because they know this particular fact: Michigan Tech has historically had excellent hockey teams. Students at colleges whose teams compete against Michigan Tech would probably be able to supply the missing word, too, though not as quickly or with as much assurance. Students at schools which do not have hockey teams, or students who have no interest in collegiate hockey would have the hardest time of all, and would need the missing word to get the correct meaning of the sentence. The more information a reader already has, the less information need be encoded in the actual passage.

The more the reader knows, the easier it is to fill in missing information, to pick up inferences, and to locate main ideas. One way of describing this process is to say that readers read to confirm or disprove what they already know; reading can be described by the phrase, *the reduction of uncertainty.*[5]

What Happens When a Reader Reads (Or Fails to Read)

Readers rely on various language cues while reading. In reading all textual materials, good readers simultaneously use cues available in the syntactic (grammatical) structures of the passage, the grapho-phonic system (the relationship of written symbols to sound), and the semantic (meaning) system. Moreover, in their search for a correct reconstruction of the author's message, good readers constantly ask themselves, "Does this make sense?" If momentarily thwarted, successful readers stop, check, and recheck all three cueing systems for further help.[6]

Consider, for example, the mystery novel. The reader reads it to answer the question, "Whodunit?" To find the solution to the murder and reduce the uncertainty, the reader is likely to hypothesize and test hypotheses along the way. This same operation happens in less obvious ways as well. Research shows that good readers continually ask questions and test hypotheses as they read all kinds of materials, using language signals left by the author to prompt a change in their hypotheses. Imagine the following sentence is from a paragraph on animal behavior:

> Lemmings do not march to the sea and throw themselves over the cliffs in mass suicide.

One word, *not*, makes all the difference in the sentence's meaning: a reader reading with the preconceived idea that lemmings *do* throw themselves into the sea is likely to completely misunderstand the sense of the sentence. A writer who wishes to make the meaning clear recognizes that the readers read with preconceptions and should give signals to mark a divergence from what the reader probably already believes:

> Contrary to popular opinion, lemmings do not march to the sea and throw themselves over the cliff in mass suicide.
>
> Lemmings do NOT march to the sea and throw themselves over the cliff in mass suicide.
>
> Although many myths have developed around the supposedly suicidal behavior of lemmings, lemmings do not in fact throw themselves over cliffs in efforts at mass destruction.

Words and phrases like *contrary to popular opinion,* the emphatic *NOT* as opposed to the simple *not, although many myths have developed, supposedly,* and *in fact* are redundant signals to readers that their expectations are not likely to be met, and that they had better slow down to receive some new information.

Even so, readers often find passages too difficult for them for several reasons. They may lack the background (the "behind-the-eye") information that the author assumes they will have before reading the material. This may be a quite reasonable assumption on the author's part, as when he or she presumes the reader will have undergone certain preparation before reading the text. But if an author makes the assumption unadvisedly, then he or she may not supply enough signposts to meaning in the forms of grammatical structure, semantic context, intermediate steps in reasoning, or background facts to allow the readers to form intelligent hypotheses about the author's principal and secondary ideas. The author may not explain specialized vocabulary clearly enough, or may not develop complex concepts in carefully defined or logically related steps. Such written material might be fine for advanced or even average students, but for the very poor student it will represent an insurmountable obstacle. The expert in the field (the instructor) often knows very little about what the beginner brings in the way of background. Since the expert already possesses more than enough "behind-the-eye" information to make logical connections, textbooks are often chosen without adequate understanding of the barriers the novice will encounter when reading them.

People assessing how readable a text is usually equate long sentences with difficult reading and short sentences with easy reading,[7] but it seems not so much to matter how long sentences are, but rather how *predictable* they are. Thus short, terse sentences packed with technical vocabulary which are not set in a redundant context—a context which repeats enough information to be predictable—will be more difficult to read than will a very long, grammatically complex sentence in which the words are familiar and the order predictable.[8]

Read, for example, the following written versions of the same information:

1. Cross-modal transfer and ipsimodal stimuli facilitate comprehension.

2. Most people will comprehend more if what they learn is presented through a variety of modes. (Modes are simply the means by which perceptions are transmitted: vision, hearing, touch, and muscular movement.) Many children do seem to prefer one mode over another, as in the case of the child who easily learns to play the piano by ear (the aural mode), but who has difficulty playing from written music (the visual mode). In most cases, however, children benefit from receiving information through a variety of senses. Information can also sometimes be presented in different forms of the same mode, as when a written story contains a picture illustrating an event described in the story. In this case, the written words and the picture represent *ipsimodal stimuli:* two reinforcing forms of the same (visual) mode.

The second passage is clearly more understandable to the novice in educational psychology than is the short sentence in the first version. Although the second passage contains far more syntactically complex sentences, the first sentence is the most difficult, paradoxically, because of its compact, declarative form which does not provide the background necessary for a beginner to understand it. An expert would likely become impatient with the laborious explanation in the second passage. Readers' ability to master the first sentence should grow as they become more proficient in the subject matter and as they gain more experience as readers.

The Three Levels of Reading Comprehension

More, however, is required of a successful reader than simple, factual comprehension. *Literal* comprehension must accompany the ability to see the implied relationships between fact, information, and the ideas of the author, and this *interpretive* or *inferential* level of comprehension should, in turn, lead to the most sophisticated reading level—the *applied* or *critical* level.[9] *Literal* reading is easy compared to the other levels, yet the reader must master it to reach the other two levels of understanding. Most college instructors assume that students are capable of these higher levels of thought without realizing that most of them do not even read for more than the main idea and a few supporting facts, that often they misunderstand the main idea or oversimplify it beyond recognition, and that they cannot organize the supporting facts rationally. Many students are simply unable to achieve literal comprehension. An instructor who begins discussing applications of a reading without making certain that the students understand the factual content is asking for trouble.[10] Requiring students to keep reading notes in a notebook throughout the course is one way to monitor and encourage at least literal comprehension.

Lucille Strain shows that readers demonstrate mastery of *literal* comprehension by doing such things as:

1. Identifying appropriate meanings for words in a selection
2. Following directions
3. Recalling sequences of events or ideas
4. Locating answers in the text to specific questions
5. Summarizing the main idea of a selection
6. Associating the text with pertinent illustrations
7. Following the sequence of the plot
8. Identifying ideas

Readers demonstrate that they are deriving *interpretive* or *inferred* meaning by:

1. Drawing logical conclusions
2. Predicting outcomes
3. Describing relationships
4. Suggesting other appropriate titles for the passage
5. Identifying the implied traits of a character[11]

Without denying the importance or difficulty of gathering, processing, and ordering information, a reader's true task is often more than these processes. Readers must confirm more than their correct perception of the author's literal and implied message. The reader must know "when to select material, how to select it, and how to determine its reliability."[12] These abilities belong to the ability to think and read critically. *Critical reading,* the correct assessment of written statements,[13] still relies on the fundamental application of confirmation or rejection by testing, verifying, and applying.[14]

Reading Questions

When initially assigning reading material, instructors can help students comprehend the assignment on all three levels if the instructor asks questions which require evidence of *literal, interpretive,* and *applied* knowledge. These questions—whether handed out in written form, or given more casually as points to think over while reading— should emphasize more than literal comprehension, particularly in college classes, although the instructor should include questions about important or often misunderstood facts. (For example, "What common misconception exists about lemmings?")

The instructor may require the answers to be written down and handed in or simply noted in the text. Under no circumstances should the student copy the answer directly from the textbook, or underline the pertinent passage in the text. Instead, the reader should rephrase the answer in his or her own words, since to rephrase the answer in one's own language requires the *decoding* of information, while copying or (worse) underlining it merely identifies the information. If we read the sentence *"The foziwugs skittered sasambly autoy,"* we would presumably have little difficulty with the question "What did the foziwugs do?" by writing the sentence "They skittered sasambly autoy." Of course they did; the syntax of the sentence makes that perfectly obvious; but if we were required to explain the action in our own words, we would be forced to contemplate the actions of foziwugs far more seriously.

College students usually try to do what the instructor wants. If they believe the instructor requires memorizing facts, they will memorize facts; if they believe they must read only for vaguely-formed main ideas, they will do that; if they believe that the instructor consistently expects a firm grasp of factual information, and wants that information to be interpreted and applied in a mature manner, they will try to achieve that. Instructors, of course, must devise questions which will develop their ability to generalize from facts. A good rule of thumb when devising questions is to consider Strain's behavioral evidence of comprehension and use the following general questions as guidelines:

What is happening? Why is it happening? How does it apply to other concepts we have studied?

Weaver and Shonkoff[15] have shown that an instructor who asks questions requiring inference and application does promote a deeper understanding of the subject on the student's part. (Students appreciate reading questions—if my own experience is any clue.) We would like to think that all this work on the instructor's part to devise significant questions would help the average student to invent superior questions for reading. This is not the case, however. Research shows teachers' questions are significantly superior to students' questions in improving reading and course comprehension.[16] This was true even when students received special question-asking instruction, when they had studied the subject for a considerable time, and when the evaluator was not the person originally posing the questions. The key, it seems to me, is the teacher's foreknowledge of what will *later* be significant versus the students' necessarily more limited perception. Students, as they become more expert in a particular subject, should slowly improve in their ability to pose significant questions, but teachers play a vital—and often unrecognized—role in guiding their students to improved reading comprehension.

Testing

Why has a student failed to read material adequately? Frequently, instructors want to send a problem reader over to the school's reading lab for "some kind of test" which can quantifiably determine what is wrong. Instructors should realize that most reading tests are hardly the precise, scientific measurements that outsiders assume them to be.[17] The word *diagnostic* implies that these tests will tell the instructor what is wrong; the word *achievement* suggests that they will accurately gauge students' abilities. In other words, the test should indicate more than just that Jane Jones is reading on the "5.4 level." It should point out that she has a poor ability to predict syntactic structure, a low comprehension of fiction, a better comprehension of factual material, and doesn't know what to do when she gets stuck on an unknown word. Most tests will not come close to diagnosing a student's problems or accurately assessing a student's achievement.

Achievement tests and most diagnostic tests break the reading process into a group of subskills or separate skills that a reader uses to decode the words on the page. These subskills are usually identified as rate (speed in words-per-minute), word-attack (the ability to read familiar and unfamiliar words aloud, using the related skills of phonics and syllabication), phonics (the relationship of the printed alphabet to sound, involving the knowledge of so-called "long" and "short" vowel sounds, consonant blends, vowel digraphs, and initial and end consonants), syllabication (the ability to break unfamiliar words into syllables), vocabulary, and structural analysis (the ability to put words together using roots, prefixes, and suffixes). Comprehension is usually listed as merely one of several subskills.

The trouble with isolating and testing for individual subskills, with comprehension simply one of a group, is that these skills are not used in isolation. They depend on each other, and thus a reading test can't accurately examine abilities separately. For example, read this word:

read

When you read it, did it sound like *red* or *reed*? You had no way of knowing which was the correct pronunciation. What about your pronunciation of the word the other times it appeared?

For example, *read* this word . . .
When you *read* it, did it sound like . . .

You had no trouble with these words because you knew the context of the sentence. In other words, your skill in word-attack, vocabulary, and even structural analysis directly depended upon your ability to use context clues, even when you knew what the word meant. If a reading instructor prescribed a reading program in phonics or vocabulary based on your failure to read the isolated word *read* correctly, she or he would ignore the real reason for your difficulty—the fact that you did not know the correct context. Such a fact may seem obvious to the general observer, but it flies in the face of the numerous reading tests which require students to identify isolated words.[18] These include the most popular and commonly used diagnostic and achievement tests, such as *The Gates-MacGinitie Reading Tests* for reading grade levels 1 through 9, *The Diagnostic Reading Tests: Upper Levels* for grade levels 7 through 13, and the most commonly used college reading achievement test, *The Nelson-Denny Reading Test: Vocabulary-Comprehension-Rate,* for grade levels 9 through 16 and beyond. All give words in isolation, in spite of overwhelming evidence against the validity of this practice, evidence which has been mounting since H. L. Smith's (1956) *Linguistic Science and the Teaching of Reading.*[19] Most of the major reading tests, however, were written before the recent research into reading began in earnest. The Nelson-Denny test, for instance, first appeared in 1924, with only cosmetic changes made in a 1960 revision.

There are other problems. Most reading tests contain gross statistical fallacies: such as norming over diverse populations; using statistically insignificant score variations to raise or lower grade level placement by several months; "proving" the validity of new tests by comparing their statistical results with older, similarly constructed and "proven" tests; averaging comprehension and subskills tests together; and lumping all of the tests' results into a single grade-level placement.[20]

Are standardized diagnostic and achievement tests worthless, then? No, indeed. They can quickly locate poor readers who then can be referred for more sophisticated testing. Recently a new kind of test, an individual reading inventory, has been devised; it can give a trained interpreter a detailed analysis of the effectiveness of the actual strategies used by readers.[21]

There are, moreover, quick and easy ways for classroom teachers to predict the ability of a particular student to read actual materials assigned in a particular class, tests called *cloze procedures,* which can help an instructor to easily identify problem readers on the first day of class.[22] The cloze procedure is a method designed to determine how readable a text is for a specific person. We have seen that the difficulty of a certain text depends on the background of the reader, as well as his or her ability to predict and confirm information using the passage's grammatical structure and context. The cloze procedure requires the reader to demonstrate all these abilities.

The instructor hands out a fairly self-explanatory passage of approximately 260 words from the textbook to be used in the course. The passage should be one the students have not seen before.[23] The first sentence of the passage is reproduced in its entirety. From there on, every fifth word is deleted (or eighth, or tenth, or whatever the instructor chooses) and a blank of equal length substituted, to a total of fifty blanks. The final sentence is left intact. Students then attempt to fill in the blanks, using a pencil. Many students find the cloze a frustrating experience, even when they score well. The instructor should encourage them not to give up, but to use the passage's context clues to guess appropriate words, and to go back to change words as many times as they wish. (Thus the need for pencils.) Allow sufficient time for as many as possible of the students to finish, usually at least thirty to forty-five minutes.

Grade the passage. Scholars who use the results of the cloze for research purposes accept only the exact word, not close synonyms; but for practical classroom purposes, very close synonyms are good enough. Students with scores of less than 40 percent will find the textbook too difficult to learn from, and should be referred to a reading professional, given a simpler text, or advised to take an easier course. Students receiving scores of between 40 and 90 percent will find the textbook easy enough to read, but still challenging enough to learn from. Students scoring over 90 percent already seem to know what is in the textbook, and are likely to be bored by it; they should be required to read a more sophisticated book, or to enroll in a more advanced course.

Here is an example of a cloze procedure:

Many so-called "vocabulary skills" are really comprehension skills. Vocabulary is obviously important (1) _____ reading comprehension, but because (2) _____ the principles behind reading (3) _____ discussed earlier, it is (4) _____ important or necessary for (5) _____ student to understand every (6) _____ word in a passage. (7) _____ words can often be (8) _____ out by using context (9) _____, and a tutor should be (10) _____ to give help in (11) _____ these clues.

Using context (12) _____ simply means that the (13) _____ is told what the (14) _____ means by the words (15) _____ phrases that surround the (16) _____ word. For instance:

Clementine (17) _____ her new chapeau on (18) _____ head, noticing how its (19) _____ lines set off her (20) _____.

Chapeau means "hat," and (21) _____ context clues are given (22) _____ let the reader know (23) _____. Sometimes the reader must (24) _____ longer for the information:

(25) _____ woman loved rapunzel better (26) _____ anything else. [No clue (27) _____ to the meaning of (28) _____.] She swore she must (29) _____ some for each meal. [(30) _____ must be something to (31) _____.] So she insisted that (32) _____ husband to go each night (33) _____ the witch's garden to (34) _____ it [Rapunzel must be (35) _____ kind of vegetable or (36) _____.] and each night he (37) _____ enough for her to (38) _____ a leafy green salad (39) _____ day. [Rapunzel must be (40) _____ lettuce or spinach.]

If (41) _____ took the time to (42) _____ up the meaning of (43) _____ in the dictionary, we (44) _____ find the synonym *rampion*—(45) _____ not too helpful fact. (46) _____ by noting the context (47) _____ the word, we found (48) _____ much more than we (49) _____ have found in the (50) _____, and in less time. (See note 24 for correct answers.)

Stress context clues to your students.

Speed Reading

We turn now to a consideration of what most people equate with "reading improvement"—speed reading. Advertised claims to the contrary, there is no proof that the faster one reads, the more one comprehends.[25] In fact, increased comprehension usually leads to increased reading speed, not the other way around; thus comprehension should always be the chief focus of any reading improvement efforts.

Actual speed is not as important as the appropriateness of that speed to the material being read. Consider the following instance: a reader rushes through an introductory surgery textbook in an hour. Is that good? Suppose the reader is a medical student. The reader will at best learn only the main ideas of the text—insufficient, we would think, to give the student enough information to perform surgery. But suppose the reader is an experienced professor of surgery who is considering textbooks for a course. In this latter case, such a reading technique is not only proper, but advisable, since slow, careful reading would be a waste of time, and would not likely provide the overview the reader requires.

Improving comprehension is usually the main goal of any course. Therefore, all reading instruction should be directed at improving a student's understanding of the appropriate written material. It's far easier, however, to accurately measure and condemn reading speed than it is to gauge comprehension, and it is much easier to talk about the principles behind increasing reading speed than it is to work on comprehension.

Readers must work at good comprehension. It does not come with machines or kits. Readers must pose questions and form hypotheses. A good reader reads to answer questions. When background information is confusing or unavailable, the good reader slows down, identifies what kind of information is missing, looks it up, asks someone in a position to know, or correctly decides that the effort is not worthwhile at the present time.

Good reading is the interaction of two minds—the writer's and the reader's. Good teachers do all they can to encourage the most active interaction possible.

Notes

1. This introduction to reading theory and practice is fundamentally psycholinguistic in approach; that is, it views reading as a process resulting from the interactions between the brain and language of the reader and the brain and language of the author. Psycholinguistic analysis of reading is not in itself a

way of teaching reading, but rather a body of knowledge about the brain, language, and reading with some obvious implications for teaching. This approach to understanding how people read is not new, having been suggested as early as 1937 by Ernest Horn [*Methods of Instruction in the Social Studies* (New York: Scribner's), p. 154.] but it achieved its present form during the merger of cognitive psychology and linguistics in the 1960s. Specific descriptions of reading based on observed linguistic cues used by readers had been published by 1963, and were well known by 1965 [Kenneth S. Goodman, "A Communicative Theory of the Reading Curriculum," *Elementary English* 40 (1963): 290–298; "The Linguistics of Reading," *The Elementary School Journal* 64 (1964): 356–361; "A Linguistic Study of Cues and Miscues in Reading," *Elementary English* 42 (1965): 639–643]. Frank Smith's *Understanding Reading: A Psycholinguistic Analysis of Reading and Learning to Read* (New York: Holt, Rinehart and Winston, 1971) followed the outpouring of research and publication in the late sixties. It made available to the novice Smith's investigations of the relationships between reading and language, as suggested by the work of such linguists and cognitive psychologists as Jerome S. Bruner, Noam Chomsky, and George A. Miller. Smith followed in 1973 with *Psycholinguistics and Reading* (New York: Holt, Rinehart and Winston), a collection of essays which in effect summarized the discipline for the nonspecialist. In his preface to this book, Smith lamented that "psycholinguistics" had even then found its way into the jargon of educators, with the intellectual cheapening and misunderstanding that usually accompanies fashionable approaches to education. For that very reason, I believe that the novice whom Smith has interested in psycholinguistics is better served by beginning further exploration in the field, not in the numerous popularizations available for teachers, but in the parent fields, beginning with such general introductions as Ulric Neisser's *Cognitive Psychology* (New York: Appleton-Century-Crofts, 1967) and *Cognition and Reality: Principles and Implications of Cognitive Psychology* (San Francisco: W. H. Freeman, 1976), before moving on to application of these theories in Frank Smith's *Comprehension and Learning* (New York: Holt, Rinehart and Winston, 1975). Good introductions to applied linguistics and reading can be found in Kenneth Goodman's *Miscue Analysis: Applications to Reading Instruction* (Urbana, Ill.: NCTE, 1973) and *The Psycholinguistic Nature of the Reading Process* (Detroit: Wayne State University Press, 1968); P. David Allen and Dorothy J. Watson's *Findings of Research in Miscue Analysis* (Urbana, Ill.: NCTE, 1976); Richard E. Hodges and E. Hugh Rudorf's *Language and Learning to Read* (Boston: Houghton Mifflin, 1972); E. Brooks Smith, Kenneth S. Goodman, and Robert Meredith's *Language and Thinking in School,* 2nd ed. (New York: Holt, Rinehart and Winston, 1977); and Constance Weaver's *Psycholinguistics and Reading: From Process to Practice* (Englewood Cliffs, N.J.: Winthrop, 1980). Many selections from these and other books are contained in Harry Singer and Robert B. Ruddell's anthology, *Theoretical Models and Processes of Reading,* 2nd ed. (Newark, Del.: International Reading Association, 1976).

2. I offer no explanation for the oft-bemoaned sorry state of secondary and college students' reading ability, except to say that its existence is documented, and that I strongly suspect that student (and parental) pressure for fewer and easier reading assignments, the time absorbed by television, and the declining academic achievements of public school teachers who are themselves frequently poor or unwilling readers have all taken their toll. [See Lance M. Gentile and

Merna McMillan, "Some of Our Students' Teachers Can't Read, Either," *Journal of Reading* 21 (1977): 145-148; Robert S. Zais, "The Decline of Academic Performance in the Classroom and the Reading Scores of Prospective Teachers: Some Observations," *The High School Journal* 62 (1978): 52-57; and "Prospective Teachers' Reading Scores: A Cause for Concern?" *Phi Delta Kappan* 59 (1978): 635.] I recall my own experience with a class of thirty graduating seniors at a major university, all of them soon to be teachers of high school English: well over half of the students admitted in a survey to never reading any books, magazines, or newspapers, except when required to for a class assignment, and none had read more than two books for pleasure that year. Many viewed reading as a "disagreeable task" [See Andrew W. Hughes and Kimber Johnston-Doyle, "What Do Teachers Read? Professional Reading and Professional Development," *Education Canada* 18 (1978): 42-45]. In an effort to reverse the downward trend in reading scores, a number of states now require programs in reading instruction for all secondary school faculty [Walter J. Lamberg, "Required Preparation for Secondary Teachers," *Reading Horizons* 18 (1978): 305-307].

3. Frank Smith, ed., *Psycholinguistics and Reading*, pp. 70-83.

4. Kenneth S. Goodman, "Behind the Eye: What Happens in Reading," in *Reading: Process and Program*, ed. K. S. Goodman and Olive Niles (Urbana, Ill.: NCTE, 1970); Kenneth S. Goodman, "Reading: A Psycholinguistic Guessing Game," *The Journal of the Reading Specialist* 4 (1967): 126-135.

5. F. Smith, *Psycholinguistics and Reading*, p. 76; Frank Smith and Deborah Lott Holmes, "The Independence of Letter, Word, and Meaning Identification in Reading," in *Psycholinguistics and Reading*, pp. 59-60.

6. John P. Helfeldt and Rosemary Lalik, "Reciprocal Student-Teacher Questioning"; Dorothy J. Watson, "The Reader-Thinker's Comprehension-Centered Reading Program"; and Charlotte T. Smith, "Improving Comprehension? That's a Good Question," in *Reading Comprehension at Four Linguistic Levels*, ed. Clifford Pennock (Newark, Del.: International Reading Association, 1979); Phyllis Weaver and Fredi Shonkoff, "Question-Asking Strategies," in *Research within Reach: A Research-Guided Response to Concerns of Reading Educators* (St. Louis and Washington, D.C.: Research and Development Interpretation Service, CEMREL, and the National Institute of Education, 1978), pp. 93-98.

7. See, for instance, Gail B. West, "Estimating Readability," in *Teaching Reading Skills in the Content Areas* (Oviedo, Fla.: Sandpiper Press, 1974), pp. 26-33.

8. Laura A. Smith, "Miscue Research and Readability," in *Findings of Research in Miscue Analysis: Classroom Implications*, ed. P. D. Allen and D. J. Watson (Urbana, Ill.: NCTE, 1976), pp. 146-151; John Dawkins, *Syntax and Readability* (Newark, Del.: International Reading Association, 1975).

9. Benjamin S. Bloom, ed., *Taxonomy of Educational Objectives: Handbook I, Cognitive Domain* (New York: David McKay, 1954); John J. DeBoer and Martha Dallman, *The Teaching of Reading* (New York: Holt, Rinehart and Winston, 1970), p. 174; Lucille B. Strain, *Accountability in Reading Instruction* (Columbus, Ohio: Charles Merrill, 1976), pp. 203-227.

10. Norma Inabinette and Pam Conlon, "The Implications of Piaget's Theory of Formal Operations in College Reading Programs," in *Proceedings*

of the Eleventh Annual Conference of the Western College Reading Association, ed. Gwyn Enright (San Diego, Calif.: Western College Reading Association, 1978), pp. 58–64.

11. Strain, p. 215.

12. Russell G. Stauffer, "Reading as a Cognitive Process," in *Resources in Reading-Language Instruction,* ed. Robert B. Ruddell, et al.(Englewood Cliffs, N.J.: Prentice-Hall, 1974), p. 316.

13. Robert H. Ennis, "A Concept of Critical Thinking," *Harvard Educational Review* 32 (1962): 84.

14. Stauffer, p. 317.

15. Weaver and Shonkoff, pp. 94–95.

16. Jane M. Morse, "Effect of Reader-Generated Questions on Learning from Prose," in *Reflections and Investigations on Reading: Twenty-Fifth Yearbook of the National Reading Conference,* ed. Wallace D. Miller and George H. McNinch (1976), pp. 310–316.

17. Robert B. Ruddell, "Achievement Test Evaluation: Limitations and Values," in *Resources in Reading-Language Instruction,* ed. Ruddell, et al., pp. 383–386; Roger Farr, *Reading: What Can Be Measured?* (Newark, Del.: International Reading Association, 1969); Robert Schreiner, *Reading Tests: A Practical Guide* (Newark, Del.: International Reading Association, 1979); Kenneth S. Goodman, "Testing in Reading: A General Critique" (Position paper for NCTE Reading Commission, 1971).

18. Farr, pp. 33–38.

19. *Linguistic Science and the Teaching of Reading* (Cambridge, Mass.: Harvard University Press, 1956).

20. Goodman, "Testing in Reading."

21. The best of these inventories, the Goodman Taxonomy of Reading Miscues [Kenneth S. Goodman and Carolyn L. Burke, *Theoretically Based Studies of Patterns of Miscues in Oral Reading Performance,* USOE Project No. 90375, Grant No. OEG-0-9-320375-4269 (Washington, D.C.: Department of Health, Education and Welfare, 1973)], has two major disadvantages which preclude widespread use: (1) the instructor needs several hours to prepare and analyze the test results, even when using computer assistance, and (2) preparation and evaluation of the test results require skill and experience on the part of the tester. The Reading Miscue Inventory, an abbreviated version of the Goodman Taxonomy, still requires more time and effort than the average instructor is able to invest [Joyce Hood, "Is Miscue Analysis Practical for Teachers?" *The Reading Teacher* 32 (1978): 260–266].

22. Marjorie Seddon Johnson and Roy A. Kress, "Procedures for Individual Inventory," in *Informal Reading Inventories,* ed. M. S. Johnson and R. A. Kress (Newark, Del.: International Reading Association, 1965); Phyllis Weaver and Fredi Shonkoff, "Cloze Tasks and Improved Reading Comprehension," in *Research within Reach;* D. Beil, "The Emperor's New Cloze," *Journal of Reading* 20 (1977): 601–604; E. Jongsma, *The Cloze Procedure as a Teaching Technique* (Newark, Del.: International Reading Association, 1971); D. K. Kennedy and P. Weener, "Visual and Auditory Training and the Cloze Procedure to Improve Reading and Listening Comprehension," *Reading Research Quarterly* 8 (1972–73): 524–541; Michael C. McKenna and Richard D. Robinson, *An Introduction to the Cloze Procedure: An Annotated Bibliography* (Newark, Del.: International Reading Association, 1980).

23. Usually, the passage is one the students have not seen before, but occasionally, when an instructor gives a cloze based on a passage with a very high concentration of mathematical information, the dense, concise nature of mathematical writing makes it necessary to allow the student to read the entire passage before completing the cloze.

24. Answers to the Cloze Procedure: 1. to; 2. of; 3. comprehension; 4. not; 5. a; 6. single; 7. new; 8. figured; 9. clues; 10; prepared; 11. using; 12. clues; 13. reader; 14. word; 15. and; 16. unknown; 17. set; 18. her; 19. sleek; 20. hair; 21. the; 22. to; 23. that; 24. wait; 25. the; 26. than; 27. as; 28. rapunzel; 29. have; 30. it; 31. eat; 32. her; 33. into; 34. gather; 35. some; 36. fruit; 37. picked; 38. make; 39. every; 40. like; 41. we; 42. look; 43. rapunzel; 44. would; 45. a; 46. but; 47. of; 48. out; 49. would; 50. dictionary

25. Farr, pp. 44-49; J. B. Stroud, "A Critical Note on Reading: Rate and Comprehension," *Psychological Bulletin* 39 (1942): 173-178.

10 Reconciling Readers and Texts

Elizabeth Flynn
Michigan Technological University

When asked to list the reading problems of their students, teachers frequently mention that students do not read analytically, cannot distinguish between important and unimportant ideas, cannot adjust their reading to the different materials they encounter, do not seem to enjoy reading, and hence approach texts unenthusiastically. Some teachers admit that their students do not read assignments at all but rely, instead, upon class discussion or lecture.

The subject of student reading problems is guaranteed to produce emotion-charged discussion. Teachers invariably express enormous frustration because student reading problems interfere so seriously with their mission as educators and yet seem so elusive. Unlike writing problems, which make themselves embarrassingly visible, reading problems often take longer to detect and are harder to diagnose. The silence and invisibility of the act of reading make it appear a mysterious process, especially to the nonspecialist faced with lethargic students.

Perhaps because they lack a better explanation, teachers often assume that reading problems are caused by laziness—students have no self-discipline. If the cause of the problem is laziness, then the solution would appear to be firmness—more quizzes, heavier reading assignments, harder exams. However, such measures are often counterproductive. Students usually do not read well because they are unable to integrate what they read with what they already know about the world. They lack the context necessary to process the material they encounter. Often the cause of the problem is not laziness but an incompatibility between readers and the texts they are asked to read.

In order to convince a group of Michigan Tech faculty that reading is as much a matter of bringing meaning to a text as extracting meaning from a text, I asked them to read the following passage:

> Menyuk (1971) has laid out the Jakobsonian courses of feature differentiation in a tree diagram (see Figure 5-2). This shows that the first distinction occurs on the feature vowel-consonant. Vowels

are differentiated on the feature-wide, consonants on oral-nasal. The reader's attention is called to Figures 2-1 and 2-2, which diagramed the hierarchical organization of Roman capital letters. Though the two domains subjected to a distinctive feature analysis —sounds and letters—are different, it is important to notice that the general model for analysis is the same and the general forms of the outcomes are similar.[1]

The faculty members, who were participating in a three-hour "Reading-across-the-Curriculum Workshop" and who were unfamiliar with reading theory and with linguistics, were baffled. Some refused to read the passage at all; others expressed anger. Not one was able to paraphrase the paragraph. The reason, of course, was that they had no context within which to place the concepts being discussed. They had never heard of Jakobson, knew nothing of "feature differentiation" or "feature analysis," and were puzzled by technical terms such as "feature-wide," and "oral-nasal." They also lacked the immediate context of the passage. Had they had the preceding paragraphs, or at least the figures referred to, they might have been able to make some sense of it. We analyzed the sentence structure and decided that the difficulty of the passage was not a result of convoluted sentences or sophisticated constructions. Indeed, the passage would not have been difficult at all for someone conversant in linguistics who had read the preceding paragraphs and who could refer to the diagrams.

Reading materials students are assigned are sometimes as disorienting to them as the above paragraph is to the nonspecialist. If students lack the necessary background or the necessary vocabulary, they will be unable to derive meaning from texts that are reasonably straightforward to someone knowledgeable in the field. Their minds will wander when they read; they will become frustrated; they will perhaps fall asleep; in other words, they will show signs of "laziness."

Frank Smith, in *Understanding Reading*, makes clear the importance of the background of the reader in making sense of written material. He says, "Whatever readers perceive in text(s)—letters, words, or meanings—depends upon the prior knowledge (nonvisual information) that they happen to bring and the implicit questions they happen to be asking."[2] According to Smith, this process of deriving meaning involves both prediction (asking questions) and comprehension (answering questions through interaction with a text).[3] The reader, then, is actively involved in creating meaning: prior knowledge predisposes a reader to ask particular questions of a text, and comprehension results when the text yields answers to those questions.

Other theorists emphasize that the "background" of a reader includes not only knowledge of subject matter and knowledge of language as it does for Smith,[4] but also emotional association as well. Louise Rosenblatt, for instance, in *The Reader, The Text, The Poem*, calls the transactions between reader and text an "event," a word which emphasizes the experiential nature of the encounter. She says, "The reader's attention to the text activates certain elements in the reader's past experience—external reference, internal response—that have become linked with the verbal symbols."[5] For Rosenblatt, the interaction between reader and text is a result not only of previously stored information, but also of past experience, including "internal response." The totality of a person's history affects the nature of the reading event.

The reading process Smith and Rosenblatt describe resembles the process James Britton sees as characteristic of all learning. In his essay, "Language as Experience," he speaks of learning as a matter of constructing a representation of the world based on past experience and generating expectations of the future on the basis of this representation, expectations which enable us to interpret the present.[6] Britton's expectations are Smith's predictions—the questions we have about an uncertain future. We come to understand the present (or the text) by posing questions which grow out of our past experience. Those questions are answered as the future becomes the present, or as prediction is modified by the text itself.

Everyone needs to make sense of the present in order to reduce uncertainty. We cannot function without asking questions and finding answers through interaction with the environment. Motivation to read is therefore present in everyone. If readers are not gaining meaning from texts, then those texts are probably inappropriate for those particular readers; they provide no satisfying answers, or the answers they do provide cannot be comprehended. Teachers determined to provide meaningful reading experiences for their students will select their reading materials carefully, use them effectively, and make use of writing to make reading more purposeful.

Selecting Materials

For most teachers, selecting appropriate materials means selecting appropriate textbooks. The standardized text expediently provides information about a variety of topics in a relatively economical way and is especially useful in large classes where individualized reading assignments are an impossibility. The textbooks most beneficial to students provide a balance of familiar and unfamiliar material; they are at once accessible and challenging. The mix of unfamiliar material with the familiar is desirable, of course, because the textbook should be a way to new knowledge. Reading material should be aimed at what Lev Vygotsky calls the "ripening functions"; it should "march ahead of development and lead it."[7]

Texts suited to the instructional level of most students in a class are best. A useful method of determining the readability of a text is the cloze procedure (see chapter 9). Another approach is to ask students themselves for an evaluation of texts. After students have been using a book for a few weeks, an instructor can ask them to write an informal critique of it. If they are finding it too difficult or too uninteresting, modifications in future reading assignments can be made. Instructors can also ask for formal or informal evaluations at the end of the term and can use the information to make changes in materials or assignments in subsequent terms.

But even texts selected to suit the majority of students will be inappropriate for some students, since in all classes there will be a range of interests and aptitudes. A solution is to use several different texts. One professor of biological sciences at Michigan Tech, for instance, has experimented with using two different books in his introductory physiology course. His class consisted of more than one hundred students comprising three distinct groups—nursing students, medical technology students, and engineering students. In an attempt to meet the needs of these different groups, he selected two different textbooks, one easier than the other. Students were free to select either text, and all took a common examination at the end of the quarter. The instructor was pleased with the results of his experiment—he had fewer complaints about the textbook and felt satisfied that his course was tailored more closely to the needs of his students. In her essay, "Reading: A Hot Issue for a Cool Librarian," Sylvia Marantz encourages all teachers to "move beyond the single standard text in an effort to find that proper balance, that right discrepancy for each level."[8]

The selection of appropriate textbooks is difficult because texts must meet the needs of a variety of students and because they must be adapted to course structures for which they are rarely ideally suited. The selection of a textbook is often a compromise, as is illustrated by the experience of professors in the Mathematical and Computer Sciences Department at Michigan Tech. The text being used in the department's introductory calculus sequence was unsatisfactory because it was too difficult for most of the students taking the course. Teachers were hesitant to select a different text, however, because the one they were using included a section on linear algebra, while the more readable textbooks they were considering did not. After much debate, they decided to select an easier text and to write their own supplement on linear algebra. The solution is not ideal; the new text has its problems. But teachers and students generally agree that the new materials are an improvement over the ones formerly used because they are more readable.

Textbooks sometimes make for tedious reading because they tend to provide only conclusions and convey little sense of the scholar's or researcher's excitement while developing the subject. They sometimes give students the impression that disciplines are rooted in codified dogma rather than controversy. When possible, therefore, textbooks should be supplemented or replaced by materials which will be more involving. Case studies, journal articles, collections of documents, biographies, and autobiographies are usually more successful in engaging students in the problem-solving process, which is the active center of all fields. The epistolary controversies found in most professional journals, for instance, are often intriguing and convey "subject matter" in a way that might be refreshing to students. Such exchanges demonstrate that authorities often disagree about facts, about methodology, and about fundamental assumptions. Students learn to look at material with a greater critical distance. They begin to see that conclusions are best understood in relation to the assumptions and methodologies which lie behind them; they learn to recognize the problem-solving process which is inherent in the knowledge they are asked to master.

Textbooks, journal articles, case studies, collections of documents, biographies, and autobiographies are written in what James Britton calls the "transactional" mode—the language to get things done: to inform, or to advise, persuade, or instruct.[9] Where possible, students should also be provided reading materials written in the "expressive" mode—language used for the purposes of exploration and discovery. Journals, diaries, and personal letters reveal the private dimension of productive activity. Students of biology, for instance, will no doubt be impressed by the delight Darwin took in seemingly trivial findings as described in his journal. Students struggling with the novels of Virginia Woolf might appreciate passages in *A Writer's Diary* which describe her difficulties in composing the novels. Expressive materials such as these serve to demystify knowledge. Students can be easily intimidated by the polished prose of transactional writing. If they are introduced to writing of the professionals which is unfinished and meandering, they will be better able to accept their own imprecision and uncertainty as well as appreciate the process whereby precision in language is achieved. Ken Macrorie in *Searching Writing* discusses the benefits students can derive from viewing the exploratory processes of the "experts." He says, "if students were to see the experts at work—

finding needs in their own lives and answering them, working
brilliantly, working stupidly, making mistakes, stumbling into profitable answers—they would understand the true nature of productive
men and women, and would come to believe that they might become
such people themselves."[10]

Using Materials

Expressive and transactional reading can be used in very different ways.
Usually, students will read diaries and letters without prodding because the materials themselves are engrossing and accessible. It is
probably not necessary, therefore, to prepare students for such reading
or even to assess their comprehension of it. Students might simply be
asked to keep a reading journal in which they respond to their reading
in some meaningful way. By examining these journals from time to
time, teachers can quickly and easily provide feedback on student
reading. Transactional materials present more problems, however.
Such materials are, by definition, further removed from personal experience and so more difficult to comprehend. A useful approach is
to employ both prereading strategies and reading strategies as a way of
insuring that students bring an appropriate context to their reading.

Prereading Strategies

Preparation for reading transactional materials can take a number of
different forms. Teachers might introduce students to material by
pointing out its specific features; go over difficult vocabulary and
graphics encountered in reading; have students write journal entries
on topics to be covered in reading; lecture on material before students
encounter similar material in a textbook; conduct discussions of
material in advance of asking students to read about a particular topic,
or allow students to discuss the topic in small groups; provide study
questions.

   The very appearance of textbooks can intimidate students; chapter
headings and subheadings may appear unfamiliar and threatening.
Instructors can lessen student resistance to new materials by introducing them to the text, pointing out useful aids such as glossaries and
study questions, providing information about the author and explaining how the text will be used in the course. Margaret Pigott in "Who's
Afraid of the Wicked Witch? Reading for College Students,"[11] recounts
her experience teaching an essay from *The New Republic*, a periodical
which, she discovered, was unfamiliar to most of the students in her
honors composition class. She lessened their anxieties by having them

leaf through an issue of the magazine, feel the texture of the paper, look closely at the pictures and advertisements, and examine the organization of the entire magazine.

It is often helpful, too, to introduce students to difficult terminology before they encounter it in a text. If textbooks do not provide glossaries of terms, teachers can prepare their own, or have students look up words they anticipate will give them difficulty. Richard Muelder in "Reading in a Mathematics Class" suggests that glossaries which students create can be organized into units so that words can be readily located. Writing definitions of words, Muelder feels, increases the retention of meaning.[12]

Teachers can also discuss graphs and charts that students will encounter in forthcoming chapters. Graphics are meant to complement printed material, but students will frequently ignore them if they appear complicated or if no one has taught the students how to read them. One approach is to have students convert graphs or charts into written explanations. The activity of writing about visual information will help students to develop ways of understanding it and enable teachers to identify problems students are having.

Writing can be used as a prereading strategy in other ways as well. Students can be asked to explore topics in journals before they read about them in their texts. Students in an introductory psychology course, for instance, might be asked to prepare for a chapter on Freudian psychology by explaining to themselves their present understanding of Freud's theories in their journals. The process of writing will trigger associations and bring to the surface a context which had previously been dormant. Journal entries may be written in class or at home and can address questions which are either directive or open-ended.

Another way of preparing students for their reading assignments is to lecture on material before it is encountered in a text. The lecture will make students more receptive to the ideas contained in assigned reading and will alert them to topics the instructor thinks are especially important. It will provide a context for reading. Students of American history, for example, will have an easier time with a chapter on the Great Depression if they are provided an outline of significant occurrences of the era beforehand. If students understand that they will have to make use of knowledge derived from their reading in postreading activities such as essays or discussion, they will be unlikely to use the outline or other study aid as a substitute for careful reading of the chapter itself.

Discussions conducted prior to reading serve a similar purpose. The exchange of ideas will produce unanswered or partially answered questions, and students will be motivated to read their texts carefully in order to find answers to those questions. Small group discussions have the added advantages of allowing for the participation of a greater number of students. Like the activity of writing in a journal, involvement in a discussion activates the memory and so allows already existing knowledge and interests to surface. In conversation, students also have the benefit of a responding audience and can receive immediate feedback on their ideas. The activity of conversing is good preparation for the much harder task of communicating with absent authors, who have only the printed page to convey their silent messages.

Study questions are another useful form of preparation. A few carefully selected questions will help students focus their reading and distinguish between significant and insignificant detail. Questions might reflect what Benjamin Bloom calls the three levels of comprehension: the literal level (what the passage says); the interpretive level (what it means); and the applied level (how it relates to other knowledge).[13] Before asking students to read Emily Dickinson's poem, "The Mountains Grow Unnoticed," for example, it might be useful to give them questions which will test all three levels of comprehension. Students might be asked to explain the nature of the contrast established by the poem (literal level); to explain why the mountains are said to have "eternal faces" (interpretive level); and to discuss ways in which the treatment of the sun in this poem differs from the treatment of it in poems previously studied (applied level). Answers need not necessarily be written out. Often the questions alone are enough to direct reading in fruitful ways.

Questions can help students better understand science texts as well. A passage on Newton's first law of motion, for example, will no doubt be read more meaningfully if students are provided study questions in advance of their reading it. Students might be asked: What is needed in order to vary either the speed or the direction of the motion of an object? (literal level); What might be some examples of an "unbalanced force"? (interpretive level); How does Newton's first law of motion help us explain the concept of centrifugal force? (applied level). The kinds of study questions provided can be determined by the sophistication of the students. Less able readers can be given a preponderance of questions on a literal level whereas advanced students will be better able to handle questions on an applied level.

Other ways of insuring that students bring the necessary background and interest to their reading include using audiovisual materials such as films, tapes, slides, and recordings. Field trips can serve a similar purpose. All of these approaches create a context for reading and stimulate interest so that assignments are approached with eagerness rather than lethargy. It is important to remember, however, that all of these approaches may also be effective *as* students are reading or *after* they have read. Students who have sufficient knowledge to handle material and who are highly motivated should not be restrained from reading. Prereading strategies are necessary only when background or motivation are deficient.

Reading Strategies

In addition to preparing students to read particular assignments, teachers can also teach students skills which they can apply to a variety of different materials in a variety of different situations. Teachers in all disciplines can take time out from their normal activities and teach students ways of handling unfamiliar vocabulary and ways of analyzing passages.

Vocabulary

Students can be taught to use context clues in order to determine the meaning of words. Such cues can be either syntactic or semantic. Syntactic cues include the placement of the word in a sentence, the form in which the word is presented, and the signal words attached to it.[14] Students can determine the part of speech of a word from syntactic cues and such information can aid in predicting meaning. In the sentence, "The microphone is an audio transducer, converting electrical signals into sound waves," for example, the syntax of the sentence tells us that "transducer" is a noun. Three clues are useful in determining the part of speech of the word: (1) The "er" suffix is often a noun ending; (2) the word's positioning after the verb "is" suggests that it is either a predicate nominative or a predicate adjective; (3) the article "an" eliminates predicate adjective as an option, and so the word must be a predicate nominative or noun. Semantic cues can aid further in determining meaning. The word "transducer" is surrounded by other words which limit it semantically. We learn from the sentence that a microphone is a kind of transducer, one which converts electrical signals into sound waves, and so we infer that transducers are converters of sorts.

Students can also be taught to determine the meanings of words by analyzing their structures. If we examine the components of the word "transducer," for instance, we see the prefix "trans," which means "across," and the root, "duce," which derives from the Latin "ducere," which means "to lead." This information supports our contention that transducers convert or lead electrical signals from one system to another. A useful tool in analyzing the structure of words is Borror's *Dictionary of Word Roots and Combining Forms.*[15] Such a work is most helpful if students learn to use it as they encounter difficult words. Isolated exercises on the meanings of word parts are not likely to enhance vocabulary development.

A dictionary is indispensable to vocabulary enrichment, but many students do not know how to use one. They are confused by the pronunciation key, by information about word etymologies, and they have little faith that a dictionary will solve their spelling problems. Teachers can show students how to use a dictionary by using it frequently as new words are encountered in class. They can demonstrate that a dictionary is most helpful after context cues and word structures have been examined. The dictionary can substantiate hunches about meanings or spellings which have resulted from different analytical methods.

Analysis

Frequently students also need help in learning to analyze the material in their textbooks. They often have difficulty determining the main idea of a passage or distinguishing between main ideas and subordinate ideas. One way of assessing students' ability to recognize hierarchical relationships is to isolate a passage from a textbook (a page or two), read it aloud, and ask them to paraphrase it. If they do so inadequately, they need help in interpreting material.

A solution is to isolate a paragraph from a passage and have students identify its main idea and relate that main idea (stated or implied) to other ideas in the paragraph. They can demonstrate those relationships graphically through the use of a tree diagram (see chapter 3) or an outline. A visual representation helps students conceptualize hierarchical relationships and helps teachers identify reading difficulties. Newton's first law of motion, for instance, might be tree diagramed as follows:

Newton's first law of motion is: Every object continues in its state of rest or of uniform motion along a straight line unless it is compelled by an outside force to change that state.

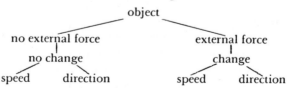

After students have learned to analyze paragraphs, they might then be encouraged to analyze entire essays. The instructor might demonstrate the approach by putting a diagram of an essay on the board, being careful to explain relationships fully. Students might then analyze an essay of their own choice, either on their own or in small groups. Frequent repetition of this practice enhances students' ability to condense large units of writing into a few key concepts and also to identify the relationship between key concepts and other less essential material. The result should be more efficient reading.

Entire books can be examined analytically, as Mortimer Adler and Charles Van Doren illustrate in their *How To Read a Book*.[16] Part Two of the book, entitled "The Third Level of Reading: Analytical Reading," suggests procedures that elaborate the idea of identifying the central thesis of an essay. Adler and Van Doren recommend "pigeon-holing a book" (classifying it), "x-raying" a book (identifying its central theme), identifying key terms, identifying propositions which make up arguments, and criticizing a book fairly. These various activities represent the most advanced level of reading. Mastery of them is a sure sign of maturity and independence.

Analytical skills can be reinforced through the use of texts designed to teach reading. Anne Eisenberg's *Reading Technical Books*, for instance, focuses on the analytical skills useful in technical courses. In addition to chapters on building technical vocabulary skills and on using a textbook effectively, it has chapters on frequently used patterns, such as examples, contrast, and cause-effect, and a chapter on "Writing Out Main Ideas." Donald E. P. Smith's *Learning to Learn* introduces students to the "SQ4R" method of reading—predicting meaning by surveying material, formulating questions about it, reading it, answering questions on it, writing questions and answers on the material, and reviewing it. The approach involves prereading, reading, and post-reading strategies: concepts are assimilated through repetition and reinforcement.[17]

Writing and Reading

Carefully integrating writing and reading assignments can also have a positive effect on student reading. Prereading strategies are helpful in preparing students for reading assignments; reading strategies are useful as students are reading difficult material; writing assignments are helpful in clarifying what has already been read. Through writing, students gain a fuller understanding of their reading. Writing assignments can range from informal journal entries to formal research papers. In all forms, writing forces readers to define ideas clearly and so results in fuller comprehension. Writing necessitates rereading and rethinking. Material is not simply ingested; it is digested.

Several professors of biological sciences at Michigan Tech have successfully integrated reading and writing assignments in order to prepare students to write effective lab reports. The procedure they employ, which involves critiquing an article from a professional journal, has resulted in lab reports which reflect an understanding of the nature of scientific discourse. Students first analyze an article from a professional journal selected by the instructor for its accessibility to undergraduates. The analysis, which is done during the lab session by students working in groups of three or four, is followed by a critique of the article by the instructor. Next, written critiques of an article selected by one of the members of the student group are prepared and then shared at the lab session. Classmates provide feedback; the papers are revised and submitted to the instructor for a grade. The approach introduces students to the relationship between scientific methodology and scientific writing. Students learn that discussions of scientific data are not simply accumulations of factual data but, rather, carefully integrated analyses of causal relationships. After students have grasped the formal characteristics of scientific writing, especially the way in which data are analyzed in the discussion section of a journal article, they are ready to prepare their own reports.

Research papers are another potentially useful writing assignment which can aid in reading development. Such papers provide an opportunity for students to explore a topic on their own, usually one which interests them, and to select their own reading materials. The assignment would seem to encourage active reading because students themselves make so many of the decisions which have a bearing on the reading they will do. Only very advanced readers are able to handle the freedom provided by the research paper assignment, however. The multiplicity of potentially useful texts can be overwhelming. Each document must be read, analyzed, evaluated, and then related to other data. The process involves highly sophisticated cognitive activity.

Writing can help students make sense of their research. It is useful early in the project, for instance, to have students define the process they have employed thus far. They can describe the sources they have consulted; they can defend the decisions they have made about those sources; and they can express their frustrations. Such papers can be extremely useful to instructors anxious to make the project as meaningful as possible. Teachers can reward students who seem to have their research under control and suggest materials and strategies to students who are frustrated. These papers need not be graded since they are best conceived of as expressive (exploratory) rather than transactional writing.

It may also be helpful to simplify the research process by dividing it into stages and requiring students to write several shorter papers rather than a single long paper. Many research papers employ a problem-solving format. The first part of the paper defines a problem and the second suggests solutions to those problems. If students write a short paper focusing on the problem definition, receive feedback on this paper both from the instructor and peers, and then revise it, they will be better prepared to proceed to the second stage in the process, the exploration of solutions. Their subsequent reading will be more focused because it will be more purposeful; research conducted after the problem has been defined will serve to confirm or refute a carefully worked out hypothesis. After students have received feedback on the second part of their paper, they are ready to revise the entire paper. Their writing will have helped them select their materials and also analyze and evaluate those materials.

In a literate society, reading is an indispensable way of making sense of the world. Motivation to read will be high if the printed word promises clarification of the environment—reduction of uncertainty and doubt. Most students are neither lazy nor recalcitrant. They resist that which cannot be integrated with past experience and embrace that which yields new insights. An important charge of teachers of all disciplines is to eliminate barriers to reading by reconciling readers and texts.

Notes

1. Eleanor J. Gibson and Harry Levin, *The Psychology of Reading* (Cambridge, Mass.: The MIT Press, 1975), p. 115.

2. Frank Smith, *Understanding Reading*, 2nd ed. (New York: Holt, Rinehart and Winston, 1978), p. 158.

3. Smith, p. 66.

4. Smith, p. 5.

5. Louise M. Rosenblatt, *The Reader, The Text, The Poem: The Transactional Theory of the Literary Work* (Carbondale: Southern Illinois University Press, 1978), p. 11.

6. James Britton, ' Language as Experience," in *Language as a Way of Knowing: A Book of Readings*, ed. Martin Nystrand (Toronto: The Ontario Institute for Studies in Education, 1977), p. 39.

7. Lev S. Vygotsky, *Thought and Language*, ed. and trans. Eugenia Hanfmann and Gertrude Vakar (Cambridge, Mass.: The MIT Press, 1962), p. 104.

8. Sylvia Marantz, "Reading: A Hot Issue for a Cool Librarian," in *Fusing Reading Skills and Content*, ed. H. Alan Robinson and Ellen Lamar Thomas (Newark, Del.: International Reading Association, 1969), pp. 122–123.

9. James Britton, Tony Burgess, Nancy Martin, Alex McLeod, and Harold Rosen, *The Development of Writing Abilities (11-18)* (London: Macmillan Education, 1975), p. 88.

10. Ken Macrorie, *Searching Writing* (Rochelle Park, N.J.: Hayden Book, 1980), preface.

11. Margaret B. Pigott, "Who's Afraid of the Wicked Witch? Reading for College Students," *Journal of Reading* 23 (1980): 534–538.

12. Richard H. Muelder, "Reading in a Mathematics Class," in *Fusing Reading Skills and Content*, p. 78.

13. Benjamin S. Bloom, ed., *Taxonomy of Educational Objectives: Cognitive Domain* (New York: McKay, 1956).

14. Harold L. Herber, *Teaching Reading in Content Areas*, 2nd ed. (Englewood Cliffs, N.J.: Prentice-Hall, 1978), p. 143.

15. Donald J. Borror, *Dictionary of Word Roots and Combining Forms* (Palo Alto, Calif.: Mayfield Publishing, 1960).

16. Mortimer J. Adler and Charles Van Doren, *How to Read a Book*, rev. ed. (New York: Simon and Schuster, 1972).

17. Other useful textbooks include: Donald E. P. Smith, ed., *Learning to Learn* (New York: Harcourt Brace Jovanovich, 1961); Martha Maxwell, *Skimming and Scanning Improvement: A Program for Self-Instruction* (New York: McGraw-Hill, 1969); Alton L. Raygor, *Reading for Significant Facts* (New York: McGraw-Hill, 1970).

11 Responding to Writing: Peer Critiques, Teacher-Student Conferences, and Essay Evaluation

Peter Schiff
Northern Kentucky University

Clarity often turns to confusion somewhere between students' expressive writing and the "finished" assignments teachers grade. Students are able to explain themselves to themselves—but not to us. This isn't surprising. By asking students to move directly from journal entries to psychological case studies, chemistry lab reports, or theater reviews, we are requiring inexperienced writers to submit their work for expert evaluation without a chance to test out ideas on less threatening audiences.

Students need opportunities to share early drafts with classmates and to receive teacher feedback before they submit papers for a grade. Peer critiquing and teacher-student conferencing give our students these chances to move gradually from notes and journal entries, through drafts, to final form. These aides to revision can decrease the fear of failure that can lead to "writer's block." By providing students with novice and expert opinion, critiquing and conferencing, we let inexperienced writers know whether they are communicating effectively with audiences of varying sophistication.

This chapter offers detailed suggestions for integrating peer critiquing and conferencing into writing assignments in the content areas. It also suggests how to make evaluative comments on student papers so that pupils can improve on subsequent assignments.

Peer Critiques

Teaching students to help each other make improvements from draft to draft is time well invested. When good student writers exchange papers, they can suggest revisions—a shortened sentence or a more vivid word—that add polish to an already strong paper. When good writers comment on the work of less skilled classmates, they can offer ways of turning illogical, confusing ideas into well-organized prose.

153

And when inexperienced writers respond to the work of skilled peers, they have the opportunity to read and imitate examples of well-written case studies, lab reports, reviews, or any of the many other formats associated with particular disciplines.

Teachers also benefit. Higher quality finished assignments resulting from students reading and commenting on one another's paper save time on grading. There are simply fewer punctuation errors, confusing sentences, or inappropriate vocabulary to slow down an instructor's reading.

The sharing of drafts can occur during class time or between classes with students taking each other's work-in-progress home. Critiques can involve a straight swap of papers between students, or pass-arounds among small groups of four or five pupils. An instructor may serve as a facilitator of the critiquing process, making certain students understand what they should be doing. Or, if brave, the teacher may plunge into the critiquing activity, subjecting his or her own draft to the comments of students.

Whether critiquing occurs in or out of class, between two students or among more, and with or without a participating instructor, there are two closely related ways in which a teacher can help pupils get the most out of reading one another's drafts. One way is to show students how to respond to the intellectual processes demonstrated in a first draft. For instance:

> the synthesis of data necessary for arriving at an hypothesis in the chemistry lab report
>
> the selection of details important in drawing a clinical conclusion in the psychology case study
>
> the discovery of successful or flawed relationships among playwright, director, actors, and technical specialists crucial to a drama critic's opinion

A second way is to direct pupils' responses to the syntax, wording, grammar, spelling, punctuation, and manuscript conventions through which the writer's understanding of a subject is conveyed.

To guide students in their roles as critics, teachers might provide pupils with two aids: (1) a sheet of paper on which are written questions pertinent to the intellectual processes necessary for completing the assignment, and (2) a sheet asking critics to respond to the written product itself. Instructors need to adapt the first sheet to their particular course's needs. For example, a history teacher wishing students to write a biography might hand out sequenced critique sheets (Figures 1 and 2) to be used a week apart.

Historical Biography Critique Sheet—Intellectual Processing

Author: Critic:

1. In one sentence, write out the main point the author makes about the biographical subject.
2. What details allow the author to reach a conclusion (simply jot down one or two words to identify pertinent details)?
3. What additional information might be helpful in substantiating the author's findings.
4. As a student of history reading this report, what is your reaction to the author's tone (for example: "too personal," "too detached," "effective blend of personal and objective")?

Figure 1.

Historical Biography Critique Sheet—Writing

Author: Critic:

1. What part of the paper seems to you the best written? Specify the lines and tell why you feel they are effective.
2. What part of the paper seems to you the weakest? Specify the lines and tell why you feel they are ineffective.
3. Which sentences are vague?
4. Which transitions bring you up short or leave you searching for connections between sentences?
5. Which words or phrases are vague and/or overused?
6. Which sentences have grammatical structures you find confusing or inaccurate?
7. What spelling and punctuation errors have you noticed?

Figure 2.

Critique sheets for other disciplines would present different directions. Instead of asking pupils to "write out the main point the author wishes to make about the biographical subject," the sheet might ask:

> In one sentence, write out the author's finding based on completion of the assigned experiment. (chemistry laboratory report)

> In one sentence, write out the author's opinion of the production. (theater review)

> In one sentence, write out the major recommendation that the author makes to the client company. (business administration consulting report)

Similarly, other questions could be adjusted to meet the requirements of different disciplines.

When students critique carefully and then revise carefully, the results can be impressive. For example, a student brought to class this health education essay draft on the dangers of smoking:

Puffin' Away

"Warning: the Surgeon General has determined that cigarette smoking is dangerous to your health." How many times has a cigarette smoker read this admonishment as he pulled another cigarette from his pack—and yet he ignors it. I myself choose to close my eyes to the continual stream of government warnings against smoking.

Why does an individual start such a habit? It's hard to say why people smoke, but I would acknowledge that I gan smoking because of peer pressure. The research done by the Federal Government alone shows that smoking contributes to caner particular of the lung but also of the tounge, throat, mouth & other parts of the body used in smoking. Also, Emphyzima another lung deasease can also be caused by the use of cigarettes. Smokers are usually more suseptiable to respitory infections and these are a longer time to cure especially than a non-smokers (especially if they continue to smoke during their illness.)

Smoking also contributes to bad breath and stained teeth. A non-smoker can immediately identify a smoker by the unpleasant oder comeing from the smokers cloths & hair. But up until a few years ago the non-smoker had no choice but to tolerate a smoky resitirant or bar or plane but things are changing and now such places where people congreate have disignated areas for people wishing to use tobacco.

A classmate reading this draft suggested that the writer (1) offer "some other possibilities for starting to smoke," (2) correct numerous spelling, punctuation, and proofreading errors, and (3) retain and expand upon such specific wording as "congregate," because "it sounds much better than 'a place where people gather.'" After receiving these suggestions and asking the critiquer for ways to implement the recommended changes, the writer prepared this revised draft.

Puffin' Away

"Warning: The Surgeon General has determined that cigarette smoking is dangerous to your health."

How many times has a cigarette smoker read this warning as he pulled another cigarette from his pack? And yet he ignores it. I, as a smoker, choose to close my eyes and ears to the continual stream of government cautions against smoking.

How does an individual get caught in this expensive, annoying, unhealthy habit? It's hard to say why other people smoke, but I would acknowledge that I began smoking (and I wish I hadn't) because of peer pressure.

The research done by the Federal Government alone shows that smoking contributes to cancer, particularly of the lung, but also of tongue, throat, mouth, and other parts of the body used in smoking. Emphysema, another lung disease, can also be caused by the use of cigarettes. Smokers are usually more susceptible to respiratory infections and take a longer time to cure than non-smokers (especially if they continue to smoke during their illness). Smoking also contributes to bad breath and stained teeth. A nonsmoker can immediately identify a smoker by the unpleasant odor coming from the smoker's clothes and hair.

Up until a few years ago, the nonsmoker had no choice but to tolerate a smoke-filled restaurant, bar, or plane, but things are changing. Now most places where people congregate have designated areas for people wishing to smoke and for people who do not smoke.

The changes in the above essay were essentially mechanical. Critiques can lead to more substantive changes, as in the essay of an engineering student who described the Pontiac (Michigan) Silverdome. In a first draft, the writer ended the essay with this paragraph:

Once inside, you are drawn like a magnet to look at the playing field. At first glance, this view can be quite breathtaking, a perfect gridiron, green outlined in white, appears. The end zones are silver and blue to match the Lions' uniforms. Then your eyes see the real sight: eighty thousand seats that circle the field and rise up and up to the top of the dome, which is over two hundred feet above the playing surface.

A critiquing classmate, after reading the entire essay, noted that the ending seemed rather abrupt. The next draft of this paper revealed that its author had taken the critiquer's comment seriously enough to add this concluding paragraph:

Beauty and efficiency can be combined in a building. The Pontiac Silverdome proves this by providing a comfortable place to watch many types of events. It's certain to take your breath away the first time you see it.

Neither the revised "Puffin' Away," nor the expanded "Silverdome" are outstanding essays. Nevertheless, both student authors improved upon first drafts by sharing work-in-progress with classmates. By reading one another's drafts, by writing suggestions on the critiquing sheets, and by discussing means to implement those suggestions, student writers subtly improved their communication. Such efforts were possible only because these exercises took place without the immediate threat of a grade. With this pressure temporarily removed, inexperienced writers were able to "fail" on first drafts, so that they might succeed on subsequent ones.

Teacher-Student Conferences

As helpful as they are for decreasing writers' anxieties and improving their writing, peer critiques can only offer students nonexpert opinion. If a school has a writing center, students can receive additional, non-threatening insight into work-in-progress. But what can inexperienced writers do when such tutorial services are not available? At some point student writing needs expert intervention. Seeking out additional critiques from roommates or friends, sharing a draft with one's former English teacher, or reading it to one's own family can serve as inter-mediate steps between an initial peer critique and the teacher-student conference. It is the teacher-student conference, however, that can offer pupils expert response to work-in-progress.

Such conferences need not be twenty or thirty minute sessions in an instructor's office. This information should be of comfort to teachers whose classes have large enrollments. As Charles Duke points out, consultations with students about their writing can take place in a variety of unlikely settings—hallways, cafeterias, libraries, and student lounges.[1] Furthermore, when such consultations focus on specific aspects of a particular piece of writing, they need last only a few minutes. For example, an instructor might offer to spend one office hour in the school library in order to direct students to specialized sources of data and to offer immediate feedback to student drafts. In this way, a library consultation of one or two minutes per student can let the instructor know if the class, as a whole, is on the right track on a research paper. Such a "mini-conference" can be of particular help to students whose topics are too broad, who are having difficulty finding sources, or who are experiencing problems organizing data.

Just as important as realizing that conferences can be short and take place at various locations is the understanding that not every student needs a conference. If a teacher uses consultation time efficiently, students who need it can be identified for intensive conference atten-tion. In planning effective, efficient conferences, teachers have found a number of approaches particularly helpful. What these conference methods have in common is that they use consultation time to make students do the work that will improve their writing on a particular paper. In this way, teachers can approach the conference with a clear conscience. The student, in every instance, writes the paper. The teacher does what business and professional consultants ideally do—clarify problems, suggest solutions, and evaluate results.

Each of the following conference approaches offers ways in which subject area teachers can become "writing consultants" to their students.

Student questions conference. One conferencing opportunity that students well along in their writing often find useful is the chance to ask the evaluating teacher questions about the merits and flaws of work-in-progress. For example, a history student might bring a list of questions along with a draft of a paper on causes of World War I to a conference. The instructor then has a chance to read the draft. Following this, the student asks questions bearing upon the intellectual processes required by the assignment. For example:

> Have I overplayed the role of Archduke Ferdinand's assassination in bringing about hostilities?
>
> Does starting my paper with events occurring during the Franco-Prussian War of 1871 make it too far removed from the topic which, after all, focuses on 1914?
>
> Are my paragraphs on the bloodline relationships among Queen Victoria, Kaiser Wilhelm, and Czar Alexander actually off-the-subject padding?

The asking and answering of such questions have two benefits. They show how deeply a student has considered complex subject matter. They also enable the pupil to receive straightforward advice on final revisions of a paper.

Paired/small group conference. One way for a teacher with classes having high enrollments to provide more students with closer attention to their writing is to hold conferences with two, three, or four pupils at a time. This sort of seminar-conference can serve as a forum for discussing an assignment as well as students' progress towards its completion.

In such a small-group consultation, several anthropology students might get together with their teacher to read drafts of essays on a Northwest American Indian society in which people vied with one another to see who could give away the most material wealth. After such a reading, students and teacher would attempt to state each essay's main idea in a single sentence. Such an effort might result in these three statements about shared drafts:

> The potlatch system, in which Northwest American Indians gained prestige by giving away personal property, provides a striking contrast with the modern-day North American's penchant for obtaining status by acquiring wealth.
>
> Because the Northwest American Indians needed so desperately to give wealth away, they became caught up in a competitive,

almost megalomanic struggle to demonstrate self-worth by dis-
possessing themselves of all worldly goods.

A typical meeting of potlatchers involved the giving away of
jewelry, blankets, homes, and slaves, followed by a feast during
which the host berated his guests as stingy ingrates who would
never be able to outgive him.

In addition to finding out whether their essays communicate major
points to several readers, recipients of the paired/small-group conference gain insight into several ways of thinking about a single subject.
The anthropology students employed three distinct intellectual processes to arrive at their views on Northwest Indian culture: comparison-
contrast of differing societies; deductive reasoning to establish the
conspicuous-giving syndrome; chronological ordering to describe an
important rite in an unfamiliar culture.

Editorial conference. It is appropriate to hold a student conference to prepare or edit the piece of writing that will be submitted
for evaluation. The editorial conference is, as its name suggests, a
chance for the instructor to comment on the way in which a student
writer expresses ideas: the music teacher's advice that a student shift
from passive to active voice in order to convey the power of a concert
pianist's recital performance; the law enforcement instructor's recom-
mendation that a pupil remove the first person singular that was
appropriate in a journal entry but no longer so in a criminology report;
the physical education teacher's correction of the misspelling of "appa-
ratus" in a major's study of the physics of gymnastics. These changes
do not alter the essence of the writer's intellectual processing as
communicated through writing. Editorial changes, however, do insure
that readers will not be sidetracked from considering the writer's
thoughts by such surface distractions as misspellings, incorrect punctuation, or inappropriate pronoun reference.

The editorial conference has been the traditional approach used by
writing teachers for many years. Its benefit (an improved "finished"
product) has often been accompanied by an undesirable side effect. This
is the distancing of the teacher from the student through premature
evaluation of a piece of writing, an alienation that Mary Hiatt refers
to as keeping a pupil "at bay."[2] It is usually better to join with the
conferee to make sense of unfamiliar information. Still, when used
selectively at the point just before final typing, the editorial conference
can provide the polish that showcases a student's clear main idea,
detailed development, and authoritative voice.

Colleague conference. This technique adapts the principle of
trusted expert as critiquer to assignments in various subject areas. The

colleague conference requires teachers of the same subject to swap office hours in order to discuss written assignments with one another's pupils. In this way, students can have the benefits of a one-to-one conference with an expert who will not be evaluating a written product.

Inclass conference. Courses where students occasionally work on their own during class time provide a setting for efficient conferencing. While biology pupils perform dissections, an instructor can call a student aside for one or two minutes of focused discussion about a draft of a lab report. While business management students wait their turn to use computer terminals, their teacher can check and comment on feasibility studies that may be due a week later. In introductory literature courses, too, the inclass conference is a way to make maximum use of consulting time. For example, for a short paper on Edgar Allen Poe, students can be asked to respond to one of Poe's stories through an inclass journal write. As the class writes, the teacher can ask individual students to state in one sentence the main idea of their Poe papers. When students' ideas are off-target, the instructor can urge pupils to revise their main idea sentences, focusing them on such topics as Poe's unusual wording, weird settings, or sense of the macabre. Such quick question-response sessions offer a double benefit: immediate teacher access to every student in a class and teacher-pupil dialogue in a setting where both are likely to be thinking actively about the subject.

Rewrite conference. There are times when a student may question the reaction of a peer critiquer. The rewrite conference allows the writer to bring draft and critique sheets to the instructor. The teacher reads the drafts and the peer critiquer's reactions. If the teacher agrees with the critiquer's views, the student can begin a revision even though unsure of the critique's validity. Then, student and teacher can explore together the relative merits of two versions of a draft. When the teacher agrees with the student writer that a bit of critiquing advice may not be the soundest possible, teacher and student can discuss more appropriate revision strategies. During the conference, the student can actually begin the agreed-upon revision to see if it "tests out." This rewrite conference provides students with helpful feedback at a stage in the assignment when they may be ready to attempt a final draft. Such a conference also offers the instructor a chance to spot-check peer critiquing suggestions to discover if students are actually providing help to one another in improving the quality of revisions.

Talk-writing conference. Students bring class notes to the conference. Then, speaking into a tape recorder, they do an "oral" draft of their writing assignment. During playback, students concentrate on the audience they wish to reach and the information they wish to convey. A second playback, during which pupils stop and start the machine, gives them a chance to transcribe, revising as they go along. This sequence, from talking to listening to transcribing to revising, provides writers with a compressed version of the writing process—one during which the teacher can observe and comment on students' writing behavior. Talk-write conferences can be especially useful early on in any subject assignment in which a pupil is having difficulty "getting started."

Journal-writing conference. The face-to-face contact of the conference makes it ideal for the teacher-student talk about a particular subject and related writing assignments. For example, a government instructor who requires students to keep journals might become engaged in a conversation with a student who is writing a paper on the government of Israel. At a point when the conversation seems to be breaking down or rambling, the teacher can ask the student to use the journal to express misgivings about the assignment.("I just don't see similarities between Israel's and other nations' forms of government.") This journal write can serve to focus both student and teacher attention on a particular problem demanding solution.

It is then the teacher's turn to respond—to clarify the assignment. ("What I hope to see in students' essays is evidence they've made analogies between the countries whose governments they are describing and the British parliamentary or American congressional systems.") With this clarification the student can begin to organize an essay that compares, for example, Israeli and British executive, judicial, and legislative processes.

As with the talk-write conference, this journal writing session is effective in getting pupils started on an assignment. In addition, in-conference journal writing can prevent the sorts of misunderstandings on assignment directions and expectations that often lead to bitterness when a paper receives a poor grade.

Model analysis conference. On writing assignments where the format of the finished product is very important, a problem-solving approach to analyzing models of such formats (laboratory reports, technical specifications, or newspaper articles) can offer stimulating practice in organizing information. For example, a teacher of journalism can present a student with five or six randomly ordered strips of paper on each of which is a paragraph from a newspaper article. By asking the student to rearrange the strips in the order "most appropriate" for a feature story, the instructor creates a puzzle. The process of solving this puzzle leads to a discussion on the importance of arranging information from most to least important. Such an activity can be modified for teaching of other writing formats, such as technical process directions (chronological arrangement of steps leading to completion of the process) or laboratory reports (inductive arrangement up to the statement of an hypothesis).

Watching-the-teacher-write conference. When a student is confused about a particular portion of the composing process, it can be both relieving and exciting to watch the teacher struggle with a similar problem. With a real letter, convention paper, or class assignment to write, the teacher gets to prove conclusively that very few people can draft perfect prose at one sitting. To see the teacher gnash teeth over opening sentences that won't appear, to watch the instructor's pen cross out words that "just won't do," to observe the professor's cutting and stapling of drafts in order to arrive at more effective idea arrangement, and to hear the scholar's unprintable shriek as a proofreading session reveals scores of typos goes far toward helping pupils realize that they, too, can compose.

What the preceding conferencing approaches share is their users' desires to help pupils move toward the point of offering their work for evaluative response. Feasible for teachers of all subject specialties employing writing as a thought tool, the conference used constructively by the conferee can make the evaluator's task simpler.

Essay Evaluation

Just what is the evaluator's task after students have written in their journals and taken interpretive notes, used such expressive writing to inspire drafts of content area assignments, subjected those assignments to peer critiquing, brought revised drafts to teacher-student conferences, and submitted "finished products" for grading? Lee Odell offers insight into the instructor's responsibility at this point. Odell cites research evidence that: "(1) Composition teachers can help students increase their conscious use of certain intellectual (cognitive and affective) processes. (2) Instruction in the use of these processes can result in writing that seems more mature, more carefully thought out, more persuasive."[3] Subject area teachers can adapt these findings to serve a dual purpose, helping students improve intellectual functioning and evaluating those students' written work at the same time. The medium for instructing and grading is the written evaluative comment. Such a comment at the end of a handed-in piece of writing need answer only one question: "To what extent has the writer demonstrated the ability to function intellectually in the manner required of scholars and practitioners in a particular discipline?"

In many cases a brief response from the instructor that sticks to answering the evaluative question allows a teacher to move toward

what Odell feels is "one important goal of measurement and evaluation: making statements that describe accurately and usefully students'
present writing and that have clear implications for students' subsequent writing."[4] For instance, an anthropology teacher might respond
to the aforementioned students of Northwest American Indian culture
in these different ways:

> Your comparison of Northwest Indian and Anglo-American use
> of property to gain prestige reveals you have discovered one of
> the values of anthropological study—the better understanding of
> our own culture. By contrasting the potlatch ceremony with
> modern wedding extravaganzas, you have shown the ability to
> organize unfamiliar data and to state crucial similarities between
> Anglo-American and native American societies. Your grade on
> this essay is 'A.'

> Your exploration of the psychic strains placed upon the pot-
> latcher made for intriguing reading. You do show the vicious
> cycle in which the need to give without receiving placed the
> Northwest Indian. Because anthropology is a complex study of
> human historical, physical, geographical and communal charac-
> teristics, a wider view of your subject than solely the psycho-
> logical is a worthy aim for your next assignment. Your grade on
> this essay is 'B.'

> Your narrative of the potlatch meeting reminded me of an en-
> joyable television documentary. The sights, sounds, and smells
> were all detailed in your paper—just as they are on such docu-
> mentaries. However, what is missing from many documentaries
> was also missing from your essay. You can remedy this by adding
> the human pressures behind a cultural rite to your next effort. In
> the case of potlatchers, such discussion of these pressures would
> have answered these questions: Why must the potlatchers give,
> give, give? What are the cultural consequences of the constant
> need to accrue wealth far in excess of a society's needs? Your grade
> for this essay is 'C.'

None of these comments takes more than a few minutes to compose.
Each sticks to the quality of thought evidenced by the writer. Each
offers a suggestion for subsequent assignments.

For teachers of courses other than composition who have paid
careful attention to the composing process, comments in a paper's
margins are unnecessary. Complex rating systems are unnecessary.
Only the brief, pointed comment at the end of a paper is needed—since
the instructor knows that a student has had the opportunity to take

data from class lectures, discussions, and readings, has attempted to understand that data through expressive writing, and has formed those understandings into a piece of writing shaped by peer critiques and teacher-student conferences.

When students do accept these chances to revise and edit before evaluation, they fulfill the promise of writing-across-the-curriculum programs that embrace the entire composing process. Such students use writing to think anthropology. They use it to think technology. They use it to think history. They use it to think.

Notes

1. "The Student-Centered Writing Conference and the Writing Process," *English Journal* 64 (December 1975): 44–47.

2. "Students at Bay: The Myth of the Conference," *College Composition and Communication* 26 (February 1975): 38.

3. "Measuring Changes in Intellectual Processes as One Dimension of Growth in Writing," in *Evaluating Writing: Describing, Measuring, Judging,* ed. Charles R. Cooper and Lee Odell (Urbana, Ill.: NCTE, 1977), p. 107.

4. Odell, p. 132.

12 Talking about Writing: The Role of the Writing Lab

Diana Freisinger
Michigan Technological University

Jill Burkland
Michigan Technological University

In order for writing across the curriculum to work effectively, the program must provide a strong referral service for faculty in all disciplines. This referral service is most commonly a writing lab. Tutors in the writing lab can and do serve as professional consultants for those faculty who do not consider themselves qualified to teach writing or even to diagnose writing problems accurately. In order to use this service effectively referring instructors must understand the unique position held by writing tutors working with students across disciplines. Those of us who train tutors for this position must prepare them for one of the most difficult jobs on campus.

Anyone who has ever taught in a writing lab or worked extensively with one-on-one instruction knows that on-the-spot evaluation is the most challenging and frustrating part of the job. Unlike classroom teachers who can read and evaluate student essays in the privacy of their studies, the tutor must, with the student looking on, read, evaluate, and decide on an effective course of instruction, all in a matter of minutes. This problem is compounded by school-wide referrals. Most students referred to the lab from disciplines other than English come with almost no idea of what went wrong with their writing. Referring instructors do not consider themselves writing teachers. Although they are in the best position to judge student writing in their discipline, they have very little or no time to spend discussing the process of writing a particular kind of paper. Since they are not prepared to evaluate the student's writing problems, they mark what they can and send the student to the lab for a more careful evaluation and instruction in writing.

The techniques used to evaluate stacks of essays from classes are not appropriate in the unprotected environment of the tutor/student conference. Tutor evaluation is different from classroom evaluation. After all, the students are coming from classes which are *using* but not *teaching* writing.

Both teacher and tutor see evaluation as an instructional process but in very different ways. A teacher's assessment of a student's work is usually the last step in an assignment. The paper is a demonstration of how well the student can use new skills or express understanding of new ideas. The student's writing is of secondary concern. Tutors, however, read a student paper *not* in terms of a lesson they have tried to teach, but as they would read any piece of writing for the first time. They read critically but without specific expectations.

Tutors haven't the emotional investment in the student's paper that the teacher has. Tutors have not given the assignment or spent hours teaching the material to be covered in the paper. As teachers we may get angry when we see students do something in their writing that we have warned against; we do not like to have our lessons ignored. Such teacher reactions affect evaluations and grades, and they should. The tutor can offer a different perspective. The tutor-student relationship is less threatening because grades and egos are less intrusive. Tutors evaluate papers-in-progress, not finished products. Their evaluations are not final judgments but starting places in their work with the students. Tutors read papers asking themselves, not "What grade does this deserve?" but rather, "Where do we begin in our work to make this a good paper?"

The objectivity a tutor brings to the evaluation process is important. It is also difficult. Tutors must shed their sense of grade consciousness and their own biases about what constitutes "good writing." They have to teach toward writing that is acceptable to teachers from all pedagogical schools and all disciplines. It is a humbling position, for tutors are working with a student to write a paper that will not only satisfy the two of them but will earn a good grade from that student's teacher. They must keep in mind an assignment that is not their own, standards that they may not share, and formats they may be unfamiliar with, and they must never reveal to the student any disagreement they may have with the teacher's methods or grades.

Students are likely to accept their tutors' criticisms and suggestions gratefully, without becoming defensive, simply because the tutor does not hold the power position of grade-giver. Because tutors do not give assignments or make final judgments, students see them more as helpers than evaluators. Therein lies the unique strength of this very delicate working relationship.

Identifying Cross-Disciplinary Goals

In order to describe the tutor/student process and the role the writing lab can play in the writing-across-the-curriculum program, the following student paper will serve as our basis for discussion:

Innovations of a Decade

Inventions of the seventies have gone through many changes and trends. I cannot mention every invention that was created, for that would take at least a book to cover all of them, but I will highlight on a few. I would also like to explain the sudden decrease of inventions and the people that created them.

Inventions, or innovations, as some insist, of the early 1970s, were built to make modern living much easier. The Ultimate Duck Blind was one such invention, invented in 1970.[1] A fiberglass shell built into the ground, contained a swivel bucket seat with a heater underneath. How's that for comfortable hunting? There is even one made for your hunting dog.

One-man transportation devices were a big thing of the early 1970s. Helicopter kits, underwater sleds for divers, and hovercrafts were very popular. Articles such as these were mainly available to people who had nothing else to do with their money.

Many of the things developed, we use today as very normal devices. Digital watches, telephone answering devices, and mini-cassettes came to light about 1971. Expanding mobile homes and portable toilets helped out our traveling needs. Another traveling device was the cruise controls on automobiles. Luxury items such as electric mittens, vests, and socks kept the outdoorsman warm. The Magicube from Sylvania, a flashbulb that fires without batteries, is used by a great number of people today.

The mid-seventies were concentrated more on anti-pollution devices and safety.

The "electric car" of 1975 created a stunning impact on automobile manufacturing.[2] The front-wheel drive vehicle had a top speed of 55 mph. It was powered by eighteen 6-volt lead-acid batteries, which gave the car a range of approximately 100 miles. The operating costs were estimated between two and three cents per mile.

Two inventions that protected the safety of drivers, were air bags in cars, which cushioned the driver in case of collision, and the Breathalizer Test, which determined the amount of alcohol a driver had consumed

Another trend in which energy conservation was introduced, made woodstoves very popular, and many new and different types were developed.

Toward the late 1970s, inventors went back to making life easier. In 1977, a "tiny television"[3] was introduced. The TV had a two-inch screen, that had a shade for outdoor use. Watching the small black and white screen up close had the same effect on your eyes as watching a 24-inch screen from 12 feet away. It's two antennas could pick up stations from an unbelievable distance.

Also, people were calling for things that lasted. General Electric then came out with the ten dollar light bulb. "That bulb," says GE, "will burn 5,000 hours (estimated life: five years) and use one-third the energy of existing incandescent household lights."[4] It would save a person about twenty dollars over its five-year life span.

Throughout the seventies, inventing and inventors themselves have decreased rapidly, and have been replaced by large corperation institutes mainly because the Supreme Court is making tougher and tougher standards of patentability for inventions.

Michael Wolff, an author of many articles in *Science Digest*, has this to say about independent inventors:

> A little Yankee ingenuity, years of devotion to a principle, unyielding commitment to success, and personal financial risk— sometimes it's hard to find one of these traits in one man. Find them all and you have found one of a rare breed that's getting rarer—the independent inventor.[5]

The Watermill Superfrank Multi-Hot-Dog Machine, the floating golf-ball retriever, the lifesaving escape chute, the Nothingness Battery Bicycle Turn Signal, the Solar Bottle, the painless syringe, the Kosher Ablution Groovy Solution portable sauna health kit, the Lazy Man's Sleeping Bag, the Illuminated Disco Shoe, and the Laminated Fountain Toothbrush with Barrier—inventions like these will still be around in the years to come, but they are becoming fewer and fewer. With the help of federal regulations and unfair court procedures, the independent inventor may soon become an extinct specie.

Endnotes

1. Paul Wahl, "The Ultimate duck Blind," *Popular Science*, July 1970, p. 30

2. Herber Shuldiner, "Electric car," *Popular Science*, Nov. 1975, p. 58

3. David Scott, "Tiny Television," *Popular Science*, March 1978, p. 184

4. R. L. Stepler, "$10 Light Bulb," *Popular Science*, Sept. 1979, p. 60

5. Michael F. Wolff, "Independent Inventors," Science Digest, Sept. 1975, pp. 44–47

At a recent writing-across-the-curriculum workshop, writing tutors and professors from such diverse fields as English, engineering, math, geology, and nursing were given this paper to read and evaluate. Their instructions were to assume that the paper was written for their class and, under that assumption, to make a list of the qualities of the paper that they found acceptable. They were then asked to identify unacceptable areas. Finally, they were to rank the problem areas from most to least serious.

The results of this exercise were both surprising and reassuring. Tutors and professors from all disciplines agreed that the paper included a good variety of interesting facts, details, and examples of recent inventions and that spelling and mechanics were generally adequate. Interestingly, only one person, a tutor, mentioned documentation. She found it adequate. Others simply ignored it when making their lists. The two major problem areas were pinpointed as "too broad a topic" and "unclear thesis." The first paragraph was seen as too general. The author mentions three rather vague directions the paper might take. Phrases such as "many changes and trends" and "highlighted a few" are keys to this lack of thesis. From there, readers agreed that the paper also needed work in organization, development of ideas, paragraphing, and transitions. Several readers also recognized as a problem the lack of a consistent voice. They specifically mentioned that the student's comment, "How's that for comfortable hunting?" was jarringly informal and out of place. There was virtually complete agreement on these lists, which surprised everyone involved. Apparently, we were all setting the same criteria for good writing. In this exercise and throughout the workshop, content and organization were consistently mentioned as most important considerations not only by English teachers but by teachers across the curriculum.

Given this agreement on goals, then, how can we best teach good writing in the writing lab? Most teachers outside English agreed that, when reading a student paper, they are most likely to mark errors in spelling or punctuation. As we have seen from the above example, these instructors are aware of more complex problems, but they usually do not have the time or the confidence to advise students in more complicated areas of writing, such as topic selection, statement of thesis, development of ideas, and organization. These areas should be the focus of writing tutors.

The Tutoring Session

How might a tutor, faced with a student and his paper, "Innovations of a Decade," go about tackling the writing problems it presents? In order to make an accurate assessment, the tutor must carefully take the following steps: Talk, Read, Praise, Question, and Decide on a course of instruction. In the best of circumstances, most conferences are limited to one hour or less, so the tutor must take these steps quickly.

Talk

One advantage the classroom teacher has in the student conference situation is foreknowledge. The teacher has the student in class, has probably read the student's work before, has made the assignment, and probably knows what to expect from both the student and the assignment. In certain courses, such as engineering and chemistry, the instructor also has a much clearer understanding of the content the paper is to cover and the language the student should be using. The tutor rarely has this advantage. Most tutors work with students they have never met on assignments they have never seen. Therefore, the first step in evaluating any student's essay is to talk to the student about the assignment. Tutors never simply read the paper first.

For years researchers like James Britton, Nancy Martin, Neil Postman and Charles Weingarten, Thom Hawkins, Ken Bruffee, and Peter Elbow have reminded us of the value of talk as a means of learning.[1] Classroom teachers often lament how few students do talk. These teachers understand how valuable it is for students to verbalize their thoughts, their discoveries. This kind of talk is what Britton and others call "shaping at the point of utterance."

Tutors offer many students the rare opportunity to talk as much as they want about what is bothering them about a paper, what they meant to say, and what they now see as something they could add. It really does not matter that what the student is saying may be obvious to the tutor, if it is a discovery to that student. Some students are unaware of how much they know until they start talking. Tutors often find themselves working with students who can talk for an hour, give interesting examples, and suggest unique ways of developing the topic and yet, in the end, cannot put these examples or ideas into writing. Tutors who pay attention to, take notes on, even tape record conversations are able to point out to these students how much they actually have to say. Tutors must, then, begin by trusting the students' own sense of themselves as writers.

In order to discover what these students need now, tutors must first find out what students think the assignment was, how they feel about their own writing, and what they would like to work on with this paper. Most students are much more candid with a tutor than they are with their own teachers. Quite frequently, they are also amazingly apt at spotting the real weaknesses in their own writing. They know what most of the problems are and where they occur. They simply do not know how to solve these problems.

Working with the essay above, a typical session might begin with the following kind of dialogue:

> Tutor: Can you tell me a little about the assignment?
> Student: Well, we were supposed to write about the seventies.
> Tutor: Just anything about the seventies? Why did you choose inventions?

Sometimes the student has very clear reasons for choosing the subject. On the other hand, with this paper the student had simply discovered a list of inventions in *Popular Science* and *Science Digest* and could see the possibility of focusing on scientific inventions through the decade. That made sense to him. He had limited his topic, had done the research, and he was taking an approach the rest of the class would probably not take. This is just the kind of information tutors need before making any kind of judgment about a paper.

About possible problems, the dialogue would go something like this:

> Tutor: Okay. How do you feel about the paper? Did you have any particular problems writing it?
> Student: She told us that we had to have a thesis, and I don't think I have one and I can't get all my facts in there without making it sound like a list. It's not supposed to sound like a list.
> Tutor: Let me read it quickly and see what you have.

Now the tutor knows what to evaluate in the paper. Only after having a student explain the assignment and his own problems with that assignment should a tutor begin to read.

Read

Reading ought to be a simple stage, but it is not. On their part, students are understandably apprehensive at the prospect of having some stranger (albeit a friendly stranger) read their work. Even in the most ideal circumstances, a tutor is still an evaluator of sorts, and evaluation is always a touchy business. The tutor must evaluate right in front of the student; there is no anonymity, no protection. Tutors, for their part, are also apprehensive about this stage of the session. They know that they must read quickly but carefully while the student waits, watches, and sometimes interrupts to explain what may not have even been read yet.

To alleviate some of the tension on both sides, tutors usually begin by explaining that they will read the entire essay before beginning a discussion. They tell the student that they will probably check places they want to talk about, but those checks serve only as reminders to them to go back to that section of the paper, nothing more. Then they read quickly, trying to keep in mind what the student has told them about the assignment and about his or her writing problems.

Tutors are looking here for a way to begin. They cannot hope to teach to every error; they know that that kind of instruction simply overloads a student anyway. Instead, they look for the major strengths and weaknesses of the paper. They can begin with the assumption that the student has tried to make sense of the assignment. They look for that sense and seek to work with it.

On this particular paper, for example, the student knew that he had to discuss the seventies in general but limit his discussion to something particular about the seventies, and use research to support a thesis. He understood that, while he had done the research and had limited the topic, he was still unable to state his thesis and that the paper read like one long, disjointed list. With that information in mind the tutor reads looking for patterns in the essay and perhaps even a hidden thesis.

Praise

Tutors must remember what researchers like Paul Diedrich have taught us—praise is an essential step in the evaluating process. It is especially essential in a one-on-one situation. If the evaluation is to mean anything at all to the student, it must demonstrate that the tutor can see what the student has done well. This praise can be directed at any part of the paper—the topic, the language, the title, even a specific sentence or description. It does not matter what it is. What does matter is that both the student and the evaluator recognize that this student has succeeded at some level.

The tutor working with the example paper would probably mention those same strengths that were pinpointed by faculty in the writing-across-the-curriculum workshop. The essay is strong on research. The student does have specific facts, though at least one reader noted that not all of his facts were accurate. Further, the student has carefully documented the essay. The tutor might also mention that, while the student has not stated his thesis yet, the essay does have a potential thesis in the very last idea presented—that the independent inventor may be getting regulated out of existence.

Question

With the information gathered in talking and reading, tutors go back over the paper asking questions about specific choices the student made. It is important for any tutor to know, for example, whether or not the student can rephrase passages to clear up confusion. For the "Innovations" essay, the tutor might ask the student to explain what he means by the seemingly out-of-place statement, "The mid-seventies were concentrated more on anti-pollution devices and safety." Does the information that follows support the statement? Can he think of ways to make it clear that the next two paragraphs are connected to the statement? What does he know about paragraphing and making transitions? Can he rephrase the statement itself so that it does not sound so confusing? The *idea* in the statement is not a bad one. The tutor's job is to help the student see how it can be presented effectively. Tutors ask questions about word choices, examples, broad statements. They do not allow the student to respond with vague answers. Instead, they keep pursuing the issue. If they want another example, they ask for it.

Some useful questions about the example essay could be focused on the quotation concerned with "Yankee ingenuity." It is an interesting comment that simply stands alone. The student has failed to develop it or to connect it to anything else in the essay. The tutor might ask the student why he used it, what it meant to him, and perhaps even suggest that something like "Yankee ingenuity" might also be a quality of the eighties. With these questions, the tutor tries to get the student to see what might be unique about the decade he is covering. Once that is achieved, the student may be able to find his thesis somewhere in the last two paragraphs of the essay.

The questioning and on-the-spot performance are important throughout the evaluation. Tutors must know whether the student really understands the topic, whether the student could do more with it if asked, or whether the student is as confused as the language in the paper suggests. That knowledge matters when a final decision on instruction is made.

Decide on Instruction

All of the talking, reading, and questioning should lead to the final evaluation. In this case, the evaluation has nothing to do with a grade. It has everything to do with a method of instruction.

Many students and instructors mistakenly assume that a student referred to a writing lab will get but one kind of instruction—drilling in basic grammar, punctuation, and spelling. As many of the workshop participants admitted, quite often instructors outside English mark only mechanics, for those are the errors they can most easily pinpoint. Since students may have problems that go far beyond mechanics, tutors must decide when to teach to basic mechanical problems and when to ignore them.

For example, tutors may ignore problems with mechanics when it is clear that the student is having serious problems developing, organizing, or explaining his topic clearly; this is the case with our example paper. In the short space of a tutoring session, time spent on spelling and punctuation is wasted on a student who only vaguely understands the topic he is trying to work with. Most tutors will ignore proofreading problems until they are convinced that the student has something to say and has said it as completely and clearly as possible.

The student who comes in with a well-developed, interesting essay that has a myriad of errors in spelling, grammar, or punctuation will benefit from a lesson on the basics. But even then, the tutor can only focus on major errors or patterns of errors (as Mina Shaughnessy has demonstrated in *Errors and Expectations*). We cannot hope to teach this student in one hour everything not learned in twelve years or more of schooling.

Sessions must focus on discovering general problems, encouraging the students to make the changes themselves, and giving a few rules or suggestions for revision. The students should never simply sit and listen. They should rewrite during the session and try new ways of saying what they want to say right then, not later.

Making the Lab Work

Any tutoring session will be more successful if the tutor and the student both have a clear idea of the assignment and the teacher's expectations. This is where teachers in other disciplines can help. As the exercise at our writing-across-the-curriculum workshop demonstrated, teachers are generally interested in working toward the same ends in improving student writing. We agree on the basics; given this, we must learn to work more closely together in helping our students.

Teachers from every discipline can and should refer students with writing problems to the lab. A teacher may wish to make this referral voluntary or it may be a requirement for course completion. When teachers refer students to the writing lab, they can help immensely by following a procedure similar to the exercise described. Students are generally referred to the lab on the basis of a piece of writing. If a student would bring that paper with the teacher's list of acceptable and unacceptable areas, tutor and student would have an immediate focus in their work. They could zero in on the problem areas identified by the referring teacher. Without such help, both tutor and student are forced to make a judgment on what is expected by the teacher. This is time-consuming and inefficient. After all, it is the referring teacher who must, in the last analysis, be satisfied with the paper. The more information the tutor and student have to work with, the more productive their session will be.

When a student is turning in a completed writing assignment, the teacher should be told that the student has worked with a tutor and be given a brief run-down of the process they followed. Teachers who know their students are working in the writing lab may take this into consideration, extending the due date where necessary or allowing the students to rewrite an unsatisfactory paper. Once a paper has been graded, the teacher may wish to write a note to the tutor giving impressions or suggestions for further work. Students should bring graded papers into the lab to share their results with their tutors.

As in any good working relationship, communication between tutor and teacher should not be one-way. Tutors must, in return, report back to referring teachers, explaining the work they have done with a student and assessing that student's progress. This should be an ongoing process. For as many weeks as a student meets with a tutor, there should be an active three-way communication among student, tutor, and referring teacher. At the end of a student's work in the lab, the tutor should send an evaluation of that student's work to the teacher.

There are several other ways that referring teachers or departments can help the work of the writing lab. Most basically, they can talk with their classes about the lab, simply giving information on where it is, how to make an appointment, and what services are available. More specifically, teachers can explain how the tutoring process could benefit students with specific assigned writing tasks. They can send copies of their paper assignments with students. (Students are often surprisingly inaccurate in their understanding of assignments.) More generally, a writing lab, in order to serve the school as a whole, should have examples of good papers and lab reports from a variety of departments. There should be style sheets and formats for documentation available to students from all disciplines. Teachers could greatly assist their students by making tape-recordings for use in the lab with sample papers, describing why and how the papers are successful.

Finally, and perhaps most important, teachers from across the curriculum can and should share their ideas and suggestions for the lab. A successful writing lab serves the whole school; in order to do this it must solicit suggestions from faculty and administration in all departments. These people know the needs of their own students. They should be encouraged to share these needs, as well as their problems and concerns, with tutors and administrators in the lab. Meetings, workshops, coffee hours, or lab open-houses are all possible forms for this kind of give and take.

With this kind of cooperation across the curriculum, with student-tutor-teacher unity of purpose, a writing lab can make significant progress in meeting the needs of students. The tutor/student relationship offers the ideal one-on-one learning situation, and the lab as a whole offers students and faculty from all disciplines a common ground for dealing with one of our students' most basic education needs.

Note

1. For further information, see the following sources: Ken Bruffee, "Collaborative Learning: Some Practical Models," *College English* 34 (February 1973): 634–643; Peter Elbow, *Writing without Teachers* (London: Oxford University Press, 1973); Thom Hawkins, *Group Inquiry Techniques for Teaching Writing* (Urbana, Ill.: ERIC/NCTE, 1976); Neil Postman and Charles Weingartner, "The Inquiry Method," in *Teaching as a Subversive Activity* (New York: Delta, 1969), pp. 25–38; Mina Shaughnessy, *Errors and Expectations* (New York: Oxford University Press, 1977).

13 A Select Bibliography

Bruce Petersen
Michigan Technological University

Language underlies learning in all disciplines. But language serves more than an informative function, important as that function is. *Using language promotes learning.* Students and teachers must see talking, writing, listening, and speaking as essential elements in the development of knowledge in all fields. Considerable evidence demonstrating this thesis now exists in psycholinguistic and cognitive research. The various authors of this volume, however, have argued more from the experience of their teaching than from the body of theoretical work which informs it.

The following bibliography includes works which inform, both practically and theoretically, the concept of writing across the curriculum. Readers interested in further study should also consult the bibliographies contained in many of the works cited here. This bibliography consists of sources for research and for practical classroom activities. It also provides background material for schools planning to develop a writing-across-the-curriculum program.

Adams, James L. *Conceptual Blockbusting.* New York: W. H. Freeman, 1974.
    A classic work on problem solving and invention across disciplines.
    Argues for a process approach to problem solving—changing the
    actual "functioning of the mind."

Ausubel, David P. "The Transition from Concrete to Abstract Cognitive
    Functioning: Theoretical Issues and Implications for Education." *Journal
    of Research in Science Teaching* 2 (1964): 261–266.
    Ausubel introduced the idea of using Piagetian learning strategies
    into the sciences. A concise statement of Ausubel's ideas. Important
    also because faculty in the sciences will have heard of his methods.

Barnes, Douglas; James Britton; and Harold Rosen. *Language, the Learner,
    and the School,* rev. ed. Harmondsworth, England: Penguin Books, 1971.
    Provides essays on language in the classroom, the value of talking
    to writing and learning, and recommendations on a language
    policy across the curriculum.

Bazerman, Charles. "A Relationship between Reading and Writing: The Conversational Model." *College English* 41 (February 1980): 656–661.
    Suggests ways to foster student participation in reading and writing. Bazerman draws on research in composition and reading and shows that students need to engage actively with texts.

Bleich, David. *Readings and Feelings: An Introduction to Subjective Criticism.* Urbana, Ill.: NCTE, 1976.
    A readable companion to Bleich's theoretical work, *Subjective Criticism.* Bleich here offers a number of classroom techniques to encourage thinking and writing about literature.

Bleich, David; Eugene R. Kintgen; Bruce Smith; and Sandor J. Vargyai. "The Psychological Study of Language and Literature: A Selected and Annotated Bibliography." *Style* 12 (Spring 1978): 113–210.
    An exhaustive bibliography of work in language and literature as aspects of human psychology. In two parts, the first lists "work on perception and cognition of language"; the second lists "works on the affective and philosophical considerations of language in relation to literature and aesthetics." Contains over 800 titles, indexed.

Bransford, John D., and Nancy S. McCarrell. "A Sketch of a Cognitive Approach to Comprehension: Some Thoughts about Understanding What It Means to Comprehend." In *Cognition and the Symbolic Process,* edited by Walter B. Weimer and David S. Palermo. Hillsdale, N.J.: Lawrence Erlbaum Associates, 1974.
    Shows that comprehension is a matter of perceiving the relations between items. Suggests that observers make contributions to perceiving and thinking about sentences.

Britton, James. *Language and Learning.* Harmondsworth, England: Penguin Books, 1970.
    Presents the theoretical background to Britton's concept of language development: "We use language as a means of organizing a representation of the world."

Britton, James. "Language and Learning across the Curriculum." Fforum 1 (Winter 1980): 55–56, 93–94.
    In this article Britton develops the concepts of *Learning I* and *Learning II. Learning I* is associated with transactional writing and employs language in the role of participant to get things done. *Learning II* employs language in the role of spectator to explore values.

Britton, James; Tony Burgess; Nancy Martin; Alex McLeod; and Harold Rosen. *The Development of Writing Abilities (11–18).* London: Macmillan Education, 1975.
    Delineates Britton's model of the writing process. Emphasizes the role of writing in all disciplines. Defines a spectrum of writing functions: expressive, transactional, and poetic.

Bronowski, Jacob. *Science and Human Values.* New York: Harper and Row, 1972.

Bronowski explores the role of science and the scientist in the shaping of human values.

Bronowski, Jacob. *The Origins of Knowledge and Imagination*. New Haven, Conn.: Yale University Press, 1978.
One scientist's view of language and imagining and their relation to science. Readable and interesting review of theories of language and philosophy and the "poetics" of scientific thought.

Brown, Joseph, et al. *Free Writing! A Group Approach: Toward a New and Simple Method of Learning and Teaching Writing*. Rochelle Park, N.J.: Hayden, 1977.
A collection of essays on the topic of free writing by teachers at MIT. Contains a number of exercises and classroom activities.

Bruner, Jerome S. *The Process of Education*. Cambridge, Mass.: Harvard University Press, 1965.
A description of the pedagogical implications of studies in cognitive psychology. In particular, discusses learning as a complex process developed in several ways—iconic, enactive, and symbolic or representational.

Bruner, Jerome S. *Toward a Theory of Instruction*. Cambridge, Mass.: Harvard University Press, 1966.
An introduction to Bruner's cognitive psychology and the philosophy he derives from it. Bruner argues that writing is a two way process—both directed out toward an audience and directed inward toward discovery.

Burgess, Tony, ed. *Understanding Children Writing*. Harmondsworth, England: Penguin Books, 1972.
Useful for its insights into the developmental aspect of writing and the value of expressive discourse.

Cooper, Charles, and Lee Odell. *Research on Composing*. Urbana, Ill.: NCTE, 1978.
Raises major questions about composition which invite research and sets out the central problems facing those interested in written discourse.

Davis, Frances R. A., and Robert P. Parker, Jr. eds. *Teaching for Literacy: Reflections on the Bullock Report*. New York: Agathon Press, 1978.
Anthologizes British and American reactions to the Bullock Report, a British government document highlighting the interdependency of language and learning. James Britton's "Foreword" introduces essays on primary/secondary school reading and writing, teacher-teacher and teacher-parent interaction, preschool language development, and literary assessment.

Donlan, Dan. "Teaching Writing in the Content Areas." *Research in the Teaching of English* 8 (Fall 1974): 250–262.
Advances hypotheses about responsibilities for and content of writing instruction based on social studies, science, mathematics, and business teachers' responses to a questionnaire including

queries on types of writing assigned, evaluating criteria, and locus of responsibility for content.

Ede, Lisa S. "On Audience and Composition." *College Composition and Communication* 30 (October 1979): 291–295.
A good introductory article on audience, with an extensive review of traditional and contemporary views on the subject.

Elbow, Peter. *Writing without Teachers.* New York: Oxford University Press, 1973.
Elbow's book contains important discussions of the processes of writing and of the usefulness of free writing and writing groups.

Emig, Janet. *The Composing Processes of Twelfth Graders.* Urbana, Ill.: NCTE, 1971.
The first major study of writers' processes as opposed to writers' products. Defines two major modes of writing, "reflexive" and "extensive," and argues for greater attention to the "reflexive" mode as students grapple with writing assignments.

Emig, Janet. "Writing as a Mode of Learning." *College Composition and Communication* 28 (May 1977): 122–128.
Emig's argument is central to the concept of writing across the curriculum. Writing is a unique way to learn, and it combines a number of cognitive skills. Emig defines the relation between product and process.

Fader, Daniel. *Hooked on Books.* New York: Medallion Books, 1966.
One of the earliest and still most readable calls that literacy be fostered in every classroom. Argues persuasively for the concept of writing and reading in all classes. Offers numerous examples for classroom use.

Field, John, and Robert Weiss. *Cases for Composition.* Boston: Little, Brown, 1979.
Describes fifty, intriguing, real-life problems in business, industry, college life, etc. Each requires some form of student *written* communication to resolve. The text includes a glossary of rhetorical terms.

Flavell, John. *Cognitive Development.* Englewood Cliffs, N.J.: Prentice-Hall, 1977.
Flavell's book is an informative introduction to the principles of cognitive growth, as well as a good discussion of the developmental theories of Piaget and others.

Flower, Linda. *Problem-Solving Strategies for Writing.* New York: Harcourt Brace Jovanovich, 1981.
Both a textbook and a description of a program for teaching writing as problem solving. A number of classroom activities and assignments which are useful even without the entire program.

Flower, Linda, and John R. Hayes. "The Cognition of Discovery: Defining a Rhetorical Problem." *College Composition and Communication* 31 (February 1980): 21–32.

An investigation into the ways writers define for themselves the kinds of problems which their writing will solve. An introduction to the concept of writing as a problem-solving activity.

Flower, Linda. "Writer-Based Prose: A Cognitive Basis for Problems in Writing." *College English* 41 (September 1979): 19-37.
Reviews Vygotsky's "inner speech" and Piaget's "egocentric" speech and proposes an integrating model based on student papers and recent research. A useful piece for interdisciplinary faculty.

Freisinger, Randall. "Cross-Disciplinary Writing Workshops: Theory and Practice." *College English* 42 (October 1980): 154-166.
A detailed rationale for writing-across-the-curriculum programs and a description, in particular, of the program at Michigan Technological University.

Freisinger, Randall, and Bruce Petersen. "Writing across the Curriculum: A Theoretical Background." *Fforum* 2 (Winter 1981): 65-67, 92.
Surveys the essential literature on writing across the curriculum and sets forth the basic theoretical premises for developing a program.

Fulwiler, Toby. "Journal-Writing across the Curriculum." In *Classroom Practices in Teaching English 1979-1980: How to Handle the Paper Load.* Urbana, Ill.: NCTE, 1979, pp. 15-22.
A thorough introduction to the use of journals and short writing assignments in the classroom. Offers a number of concrete examples.

Fulwiler, Toby. "Showing, Not Telling, at a Faculty Workshop." *College English* 43 (January 1981) 55-63.
Describes the faculty workshops which form the basis for Michigan Technological University's writing-across-the-curriculum program. Offers good, practical examples.

Gadamer, Hans-Georg. *Philosophical Hermeneutics,* trans. and ed. David E. Linge. Berkeley: University of California Press, 1976.
This collection of essays introduces the reader to Gadamer's conception of hermeneutics in a more accessible way than *Truth and Method.* Gadamer argues that all knowledge rests on linguistic foundations.

Gibson, Walker, ed. *The Limits of Language.* New York: Hill and Wang, 1962.
A collection of essays by artists and scientists on the power, possibilities, and limitations of language.

Halliday, M. A. K. *Explorations in the Functions of Language.* New York: Elsevier, 1973.
A study that attempts to explain the nature of language in functional terms and the different purposes for which people use language. Halliday also explores the implications of these processes for use in learning.

Hanson, Mark. *Sources.* Lakeside, Calif.: Interact, 1978.
A detailed description of journal use in a writing class. Numerous suggestions for making personal writing assignments which result

in a comprehensive journal by the end of the term; suitable for all writing-intensive classes at all grade levels.

Hamilton, David. "Interdisciplinary Writing." *College English* 41 (March 1980): 780–796.
>   A suggestion for integrating process into the curriculum of technical writing. Several useful assignments.

Harris, Muriel, ed. *The Writing Lab Newsletter*. Lafayette, Ind.: Purdue University, Department of English.
>   An indispensible newsletter for anyone directing a writing lab or planning one. Provides a forum for the exchange of ideas from writing labs across the country.

Hawkins, Thom. *Group Inquiry Techniques for Teaching Writing*. Urbana, Ill.: ERIC/NCTE, 1976.
>   Hawkins outlines theories and methods for using groups in the composition class while also engaging students in the writing process.

Hawley, Robert; Sidney Simon; and D. D. Britton. *Composition for Personal Growth*. New York: Hart, 1973.
>   Exploration of the relationship between cognitive and emotional growth and writing. Text includes numerous practical suggestions for classroom writing activities useful to teachers at all grade levels.

Hirsch, E. D., Jr. *The Philosophy of Composition*. Chicago: University of Chicago Press, 1977.
>   Sets forth Hirsch's concept of "relative readability." An important, if controversial, approach to composition, its features, and the psychological constraints on its processing.

Irmscher, William F. "Writing as a Way of Learning and Developing." *College Composition and Communication* 30 (October 1979): 240–241.
>   Argues that writing "is a way of fashioning a network of associations and increasing our potential for learning."

Kinneavy, James L. *A Theory of Discourse*. Englewood Cliffs, N.J.: Prentice-Hall, 1971.
>   An important examination of the purposes for which we use language. Contains wide-ranging discussions of the history of discourse and posits a modern theory based on the aims of a particular discourse.

Kroll, Barry. "Cognitive Egocentrism and the Problem of Audience Awareness in Written Discourse." *Research in the Teaching of English* 12 (October 1978): 269–281.
>   Kroll describes an empirical study (based on the work of Piaget) which suggests that beginning writers (fourth graders in this study) communicate better orally. Kroll argues that these writers do not realize their audience's communication needs.

Kuhn, Thomas. *The Structure of Scientific Revolutions*. 2nd ed. Chicago: Chicago University Press, 1970.
>   Kuhn's epistemological explanation of the scientific process suggests that scientific knowledge develops from a social structure.

The book is an important introduction to understanding modern scientific thought.

Macrorie, Ken. *Telling Writing.* Rochelle Park, N.J.: Hayden, 1970.
Macrorie's text is a standard for teachers who want their students to explore themselves and their relation to their world. The book is especially valuable for its description of "Engfish," and for its definition of free writing. Provides a refreshing look at writing and writing instruction.

Maimon, Elaine. "Talking with Strangers." *College Composition and Communication* 30 (December 1979): 364–369.
Maimon discusses the problems of writing to an unknown audience and analyzes the writer's anxieties inherent in such a situation. She offers a number of explicit solutions for use in the classroom.

Maimon, Elaine; Gerald Belcher; Gail Hearn; Barbara Nodine; and Finburn O'Connor. *Writing in the Arts and Sciences.* Cambridge, Mass.: Winthrop, 1981.
An introduction to language and thinking processes across the curriculum. Especially useful for its specific interdisciplinary applications. The book takes a thoroughgoing process approach to writing.

Martin, Nancy; P. D'Arcy; B. Newton; and R. Parker. *Writing and Learning across the Curriculum 11–16.* London: Ward Lock Educational, 1975.
Provides good background to the principles underlying most writing-across-the-curriculum programs.

Miller, Carolyn R. "A Humanistic Rationale for Technical Writing." *College English* 40 (1979): 610–617.
Miller argues that objectivity in science is not an innate property of scientific method. Rather, objectivity is rhetorical and relies on social agreement and internal consistency.

Moffett, James. *Teaching the Universe of Discourse.* New York: Houghton Mifflin, 1968.
Moffett argues that writers naturally (psychologically) move outward from audiences they know toward impersonal, unknown audiences. He suggests a logical sequence of writing and learning tasks which follow the underlying thinking processes of students.

Murray, Donald. *A Writer Teaches Writing.* Boston: Houghton-Mifflin, 1968.
Murray's book is a good illustration of a process approach to the teaching of writing by a professional writer and composition teacher.

Neisser, Ulric. *Cognition and Reality: Principles and Implications of Cognitive Psychology.* San Francisco: W. H. Freeman, 1976.
Neisser's book deals with a number of the questions and implications associated with cognitive research. In particular, Neisser suggests a model of consciousness based on cognitive theory.

Nystrand, Martin, ed. *Language as a Way of Knowing: A Book of Readings.* Ontario Institute for Studies in Education, 1977.

This collection provides an excellent introduction to the idea that language can serve a heuristic function in learning.

Odell, Lee. "Piaget, Problem-Solving, and Freshman Composition." *College Composition and Communication* 24 (February 1973): 36–42.
A description of one teacher's method of integrating cognitive theory and pedagogical practice. An early definition of writing as problem solving which sets out many questions only now being researched.

Odell, Lee. "The Process of Writing and the Process of Learning." *College Composition and Communication* 31 (February 1980): 42–50.
A call for collaboration with colleagues in other disciplines and a brief analysis of present work on the composing process.

Petersen, Bruce. "Words for Feelings: An Emotional Lexicon." *Arizona English Bulletin* 23 (February 1981): 7–11.
Argues that vocabulary development should take place in an interpersonal atmosphere. Offers a method for using students' response journals to test their private language systems.

Pfister, Fred R., and Joanne F. Petrick. "A Heuristic Model for Creating a Writer's Audience." *College Composition and Communication* 31 (May 1980): 213–220.
Describes a sequential method for introducing students to audience. As the writers begin each progressive assignment they answer questions (the heuristic) which assist them in understanding the needs of their audience.

Piaget, Jean. *Language and Thought of the Child,* trans. M. Gabain. London: Routledge and Kegan Paul, 1959.
Analysis of research into the cognitive processes underlying the acquisition of language. Introduces the substance of Piaget's theory of learning and his research method.

Piaget, Jean. *Psychology and Epistemology: Towards a Theory of Knowledge.* New York: Viking Press, 1971.
In this work Piaget attempts to link theories of cognitive, field, and psychoanalytic psychology into a coherent whole. He argues for a recognition of the personal psychological bases of thought.

Polanyi, Michael. *Personal Knowledge: Towards a Post-Critical Philosophy.* Chicago: University of Chicago Press, 1962.
An eloquent discussion of the role of the subject in knowing. Of particular interest is Polanyi's concept of "tacit knowledge."

Raimes, Ann. "Writing and Learning across the Curriculum: The Experience of a Faculty Seminar." *College English* 41 (March 1980): 797–801.
Describes the writing-across-the-curriculum program at Hunter College. Especially useful as an alternative to the method developed at Michigan Technological University.

Rose, Mike. "When Faculty Talk about Writing." *College English* 41 (November 1979): 272–279.
Discusses some of the administrative problems encountered in creating an interdisciplinary writing program. Offers solutions to many of these problems.

Rosenblatt, Louise. *Literature as Exploration,* rev. ed. New York: Noble and Noble, 1965.
> An introduction to Rosenblatt's theory of reading and interpretation. A useful source of information about teaching literature as a transaction between real readers and texts. Contains suggestions for classroom assignments.

Schools Council Project: Writing across the Curriculum 11-16, 2nd ed. London: Ward Lock Educational, 1976.
> A series of six pamphlets dealing with a variety of topics integral to establishing a writing-across-the-curriculum project. These pamphlets provide practical applications of Britton's theories.

Shaughnessy, Mina P. *Errors and Expectations: A Guide for the Teacher of Basic Writing.* New York: Oxford University Press, 1977.
> Shaughnessy examines the process of writing and provides important perspectives on interdisciplinary learning and basic writing students. She provides ways of first diagnosing patterns of problems and, then, of setting up a program to deal with those problems.

Slobin, Dan. *Psycholinguistics.* Glenview, Ill.: Scott Foresman, 1974.
> This work provides a short, useful exploration of the aims and principles of this relatively new and important field.

Smith, Frank. *Comprehension and Learning.* New York: Holt, Rinehart and Winston, 1975.
> Establishes the personal nature of reading and connects to Britton's theory of expressive discourse. Also provides good summary of learning theory.

Stafford, William. *Writing the Australian Crawl.* Ann Arbor: University of Michigan Press, 1978.
> A prominent poet articulates his views on what it means to write poetry and to be a poet.

Stelmahoske, I. "Correlation of Writing with Other Subjects: A Selected Bibliography." (mimeographed) Department of English, University of Wisconsin-Stevens Point.
> Bibliography of sources for writing across disciplines.

Tate, Gary, ed. *Teaching Composition: 10 Bibliographical Essays.* Fort Worth: Texas Christian University Press, 1976.
> An invaluable set of essays on composition written by authors such as Richard Young (on invention), Joseph Comprone (on media), Edward P. J. Corbett (on style), and Mina Shaughnessy (on basic writers).

Tedlock, David, and Paul Jarvie. *Casebook Rhetoric: A Problem Solving Approach to Composition.* New York: Holt, Rinehart and Winston, 1981.
> Contains short, realistic narratives to be resolved through various forms of writing. Contains extensive apparatus on traditional rhetorical modes as well as some exercise on more recent methods, e.g., sentence combining. (See also Field and Weiss, above.)

Vygotsky, Lev Semenovich. *Thought and Language.* trans. Eugenia Hanfmann and Gertrude Vakar. Cambridge, Mass.: The MIT Press, 1962.

Vygotsky's study of the roots of language and thought and of the relationships between speech and thought has become essential reading in composition. Vygotsky's concept of "inner speech" applies to Britton's idea of "expressive" language.

Weiss, Robert, and Michael Peich. "Faculty Attitude Change in a Cross-Disciplinary Writing Workshop." *College Composition and Communication* 31 (February 1980): 33–41.

Describes the experience of faculty workshops based on a model developed at West Chester State College. Outlines activities day by day.

Wolf, Maryanne; Mark K. McQuillan; and Eugene Radwin, eds. *Thought and Language/Language and Reading.* Cambridge, Mass.: Harvard Educational Review, Reprint Series No. 14, 1980.

A wide collection of essays on topics of language by authors such as Noam Chomsky, Yetta Goodman, John B. Carroll, Paulo Freire, Frank Smith, and Carol Chomsky. Rapidly surveys research and theory in psycholinguistics, cognition, current pedagogy, and reading.

Zukav, Gary. *The Dancing Wu Li Masters: An Overview of the New Physics.* New York: William Morrow and Company, 1979.

A popular review of the conceptual basis of contemporary theories in physics and their connections to religious and cultural values.

Contributors

Carol Berkenkotter is Assistant Professor of Rhetoric and Composition in the Department of Humanities at Michigan Technological University, where she participates in the writing-across-the-curriculum program and has codirected problem-solving workshops for the faculty. She has held a National Endowment for the Humanities Fellowship at Carnegie-Mellon University, where she studied rhetorical invention and did research on problem-solving and writing. Her publications include articles on composition theory, pedagogy, and cognitive psychology.

Jill Burkland is a tutor of both writing and reading at Michigan Technological University's Language Skills Laboratory. She is also a faculty assistant in the Humanities Department, where she teaches in the freshman composition series. She was formerly a high school teacher with North St. Paul, Minnesota, public schools.

Anne Falke (Erlebach) is Associate Professor of Literature and Reading and the former director of the Reading Laboratory at Michigan Technological University, where since 1974 she has taught courses in reading theory, linguistics, literature, composition, and folklore. A past director-at-large of the Western College Reading Association, she also published articles on seventeeth-century literature (prose fiction and the metaphysical poets), the Western novel, and other subjects, and has recently completed a modernized, critical edition of a Renaissance prose chivalric romance.

Elizabeth Flynn is Assistant Professor of Reading and Composition at Michigan Technological University. She has taught writing at The Ohio State University, the University of Dusseldorf, and Antioch College, and published articles on reader response criticism and pedagogy.

Diana Freisinger teaches composition and literature at Michigan Technological University. She coordinates the tutoring program in the Language Skills Laboratory and she has presented papers on the tutoring program at conferences and workshops.

Randall Freisinger is Director of Freshman English at Michigan Technological University. He has served as director of the Missouri Writing Project and codirector of the Upper Peninsula Writing Project. He has published articles in *College English* and elsewhere on composition and writing across-the curriculum.

Toby Fulwiler is Assistant Head of Humanities and ▓▓▓ Programs at Michigan Technological University. ▓▓▓ Copper Country Writing Project, serves on the ▓▓▓ National Writing Project and the Executive Co▓ Council of Teachers of English. He has publis▓ plinary writing in *College English, English Jou*▓ *tion and Communication.*

Jack Jobst is Director of the Technical Communi▓▓▓ Technological University. He has taught hig▓ ▓▓▓ and college level courses at Southwest Miss▓ ▓▓▓ University of Missouri-Columbia. He has ▓▓▓ journals and is currently researching the t▓ ▓▓▓ writing.

Robert Jones is Assistant Professor of Literature and Lingu▓▓ Technological University and is a codirector of the faculty writing wor▓ shops offered each summer. He teaches composition, linguistics, literature, and technical writing, and has published several articles on literature and composition.

James Kalmbach is an Assistant Professor of Rhetoric and Communication at Michigan Technological University. He previously taught at Michigan State University where he was the assistant director of the Department of English Writing Program. He has worked on curriculum development projects with middle schools and high schools and is currently involved in research collecting narratives about writing instruction.

Bruce Petersen is Director of the Language Skills Laboratory at Michigan Technological University. He has codirected the Upper Peninsula Writing Project and is currently codirector of the Copper Country Writing Project, both affiliations of the National Writing Project. He has published in *Arizona English Bulletin* and *College English.*

William Powers is Professor of Literature and Dean of the College of Sciences and Arts at Michigan Technological University. He teaches composition and literature and is the author (with Wallace Kaufman) of *The Writer's Mind* (1970), and several articles on composition and the composing process in various journals.

Peter Schiff is Assistant Professor of English at Northern Kentucky University, where he coordinates the English education program and teaches courses in writing and the teaching of writing. He formerly taught at Michigan Technological University, where he participated in the writing-across-the-curriculum program. His publications include articles on composition research and pedagogy, teacher training, and developmental education.

Art Young is Professor of Literature and Philosophy and Department Head of Humanities at Michigan Technological University and Project Director of the University-wide Communications Skills Institute funded by the General Motors Foundation. He is the author of *Shelley and Nonviolence* (1975) and a number of articles on composition and humanities.

Toby Fulwiler is Assistant Head of Humanities and Coordinator of Writing Programs at Michigan Technological University. He is codirector of the Copper Country Writing Project, serves on the Advisory Board of the National Writing Project and the Executive Committee of the Michigan Council of Teachers of English. He has published articles on interdisciplinary writing in *College English, English Journal,* and *College Composition and Communication.*

Jack Jobst is Director of the Technical Communications program at Michigan Technological University. He has taught high school in Omaha, Nebraska and college level courses at Southwest Missouri State University and the University of Missouri-Columbia. He has published in technical writing journals and is currently researching the teaching of graphics and manual writing.

Robert Jones is Assistant Professor of Literature and Linguistics at Michigan Technological University and is a codirector of the faculty writing workshops offered each summer. He teaches composition, linguistics, literature, and technical writing, and has published several articles on literature and composition.

James Kalmbach is an Assistant Professor of Rhetoric and Communication at Michigan Technological University. He previously taught at Michigan State University where he was the assistant director of the Department of English Writing Program. He has worked on curriculum development projects with middle schools and high schools and is currently involved in research collecting narratives about writing instruction.

Bruce Petersen is Director of the Language Skills Laboratory at Michigan Technological University. He has codirected the Upper Peninsula Writing Project and is currently codirector of the Copper Country Writing Project, both affiliations of the National Writing Project. He has published in *Arizona English Bulletin* and *College English.*

William Powers is Professor of Literature and Dean of the College of Sciences and Arts at Michigan Technological University. He teaches composition and literature and is the author (with Wallace Kaufman) of *The Writer's Mind* (1970), and several articles on composition and the composing process in various journals.

Peter Schiff is Assistant Professor of English at Northern Kentucky University, where he coordinates the English education program and teaches courses in writing and the teaching of writing. He formerly taught at Michigan Technological University, where he participated in the writing-across-the-curriculum program. His publications include articles on composition research and pedagogy, teacher training, and developmental education.

Art Young is Professor of Literature and Philosophy and Department Head of Humanities at Michigan Technological University and Project Director of the University-wide Communications Skills Institute funded by the General Motors Foundation. He is the author of *Shelley and Nonviolence* (1975) and a number of articles on composition and humanities.

Contributors

Carol Berkenkotter is Assistant Professor of Rhetoric and Composition in the Department of Humanities at Michigan Technological University, where she participates in the writing-across-the-curriculum program and has codirected problem-solving workshops for the faculty. She has held a National Endowment for the Humanities Fellowship at Carnegie-Mellon University, where she studied rhetorical invention and did research on problem-solving and writing. Her publications include articles on composition theory, pedagogy, and cognitive psychology.

Jill Burkland is a tutor of both writing and reading at Michigan Technological University's Language Skills Laboratory. She is also a faculty assistant in the Humanities Department, where she teaches in the freshman composition series. She was formerly a high school teacher with North St. Paul, Minnesota, public schools.

Anne Falke (Erlebach) is Associate Professor of Literature and Reading and the former director of the Reading Laboratory at Michigan Technological University, where since 1974 she has taught courses in reading theory, linguistics, literature, composition, and folklore. A past director-at-large of the Western College Reading Association, she also published articles on seventeeth-century literature (prose fiction and the metaphysical poets), the Western novel, and other subjects, and has recently completed a modernized, critical edition of a Renaissance prose chivalric romance.

Elizabeth Flynn is Assistant Professor of Reading and Composition at Michigan Technological University. She has taught writing at The Ohio State University, the University of Dusseldorf, and Antioch College, and published articles on reader response criticism and pedagogy.

Diana Freisinger teaches composition and literature at Michigan Technological University. She coordinates the tutoring program in the Language Skills Laboratory and she has presented papers on the tutoring program at conferences and workshops.

Randall Freisinger is Director of Freshman English at Michigan Technological University. He has served as director of the Missouri Writing Project and codirector of the Upper Peninsula Writing Project. He has published articles in *College English* and elsewhere on composition and writing across-the curriculum.